An Island Village

Colijnsplaat, North Beveland Island ~ in the North Sea ~ Zeeland, the Netherlands (1883)

An Island Village

BETH MERIZON

MARINUS PRESS | BEULAH, MICHIGAN

Copyright © 2021 Marinus Press

An Island Village by Beth Merizon

All rights reserved.

ISBN 978-0-578-99831-2

Illustrations by Armand J. Merizon

Book design by Aimé Merizon

Published by Marinus Press

POB 702, Beulah MI 49617

marinuspress@gmail.com

🐢 MARINUS PRESS

Cover image: Jasper (Jan) Merizon painted this watercolor of the Potappel Mill, his wife's cousin's home in Colijnsplaat, where Josephine (Joppa DeJonge) had many fond memories. It was framed and hung in her parent's sitting room after moving to America.

Some images throughout the book are not personal to the family although they are depictions from the Zeeland islands during the same time period.

In memory of

Josephine

&

Jasper

Contents

Family Trees xii

Acknowledgments 1

Preface: "Do You Remember?" 3

The Lay of the Land 5

Colijnsplaat 8

Daffodils and Cuckoo Birds 11

A House that Faced the Dike 15

Mostly Sea 18

The Box of Gold 21

Pennies from Rotterdam 23

On Saturday 26

The Potappel Mill 30

The Green Cart *37*

Viena's Birthday *41*

The House on the Voorstraat *43*

Homebodies *47*

Ship Ahoy *50*

In Rotterdam *57*

School Days *63*

Plaatjes! Gornet! *68*

Zee Kraal *71*

Spoon Food *74*

At Whitsuntide *77*

A Box to Own *80*

Beetles on Leash *83*

Sunday *85*

Under the Lindens *91*

The Kermis *94*

Burned Letters *99*

The Bleach *102*

A Shoe Could Be a Ship *104*

The King's Path *107*

The Bell Tolls *109*

Hunters from France   114

Pork for the Winter   117

Ice on the Moat   119

Foot-Happy   122

Round Loaves and Crusts   125

Saint Marten's Day   128

An Island Farm   130

Slanted Pockets   137

A Braid to Reckon With   139

Legend and Song   141

A Winter Kitchen   146

Saltwater and Sweet   149

Home Over the Roofs   153

A Door Swings Open   157

Farewell, Tannetje!   163

Tannetje Sends a Letter   170

The Advance Guard   172

The Skipper Sails West   176

Dutch Glossary   183

Colijnsplaat Village Map   186

About the Author   189

Family Lineage of Jasper Merizon

MARINUS MERIZON, SR.
Retired harbormaster & woodworker

ADRIANA MERIZON
Wife of Marinus

ELIZABETH BREAS
(GROOTMOEDER BETJE)
Mother of Lavina Breas

ADRIAAN MERIZON, SR.
Skipper of freighter Lavina

LAVINA BREAS MERIZON
Wife of Adriaan, Sr.

Children of Adriaan & Lavina Merizon:

ADRIANA (JANA)
ELIZABETH
NEELTJE (NELLIE)
LEUN (LENA)
ADRIAAN, JR.
MARIA (MARY)
MARINUS
JASPER ADRIAAN (JAN OR JAP)
JAANTJE

Family Lineage of Joppa DeJonge

JAN DE JONGE ELIZABETH DE JONGE
Farmer *Wife of Jan De Jonge*

Children of Jan & Elizabeth De Jonge:

JANNETJE (JENNIE)
JOPPA (JO, OR JOSEPHINE)
MARGRIETA (MAGGIE)
PRIEN (PRENA)
JOHANNES (JOHN)
NEELTJE (DIED IN INFANCY)
MARIENA (MARIAN)
NEELTJE (NELLIE)
GERARD (GARY)

Acknowledgments

*T*he source of this narrative was a rich well of shared memories, old letters, and photographs. For these I am indebted to my parents and my aunts and uncles, who lived these pages and whose recollections preserved for us in microcosm a period and a way of life not gone forever.

I am indebted to Jeanne Merizon Arnold and Sharon Merizon who generously offered to type the manuscript in its successive stages; also to the late Dr. Andriaan Barnouw, who read the manuscript with particular attention to Dutch words and phrases, and to my niece Aimé Merizon who edited, designed and produced the book.

Facts concerning the physical history of the island were provided by the Netherlands Information Service. The Holland-America Steamship Lines consulted their records to verify certain details regarding ships and sailings.

Josephine DeYoung (Joppa DeJonge) and Jasper (Jan) Merizon on wedding day.

Preface:
"Do You Remember?"

"**D**o you remember having this in Colijnsplaat?" my father would say to my mother, taking from the plate a slice of spiced cheese, or a serving of fish, or of vegetable seasoned with nutmeg. So it went on through the years—their exchange of memories of all kinds, rooted in an Old World island childhood. Their tone of voice as they spoke was gentle with pleasure and with affection for the things they recalled.

From the time I was old enough to sit at the table I heard these recollections of Colijnsplaat. Often they were amusing and even highly entertaining, but their impressions were quickly overlaid with the activities and interests of the day.

There came a time, however, when Colijnsplaat, put away and forgotten like a toy village of childhood, began to tug at my attention. No longer was I passive when recollections fell from the lips of the silvering Jan and Jo. I urged them to go on. When their brothers and sisters came to our home, or when I was in one of theirs, I questioned them, and they, too, gave generously, their eyes glowing with the warmth of memories kindled. One of the aunts living half a continent away sent long, storylike letters that took me down the streets and into the houses of Colijnsplaat and onto the dike and quay.

I searched whatever books on Holland I could find for a traveler's view of North Beveland Island, cruising with the authors the waterways of Zeeland as in a land of dream. "Zeeland," said Dürer, "is beautiful and strange because of the water." I waited, as we cruised, for a good, satisfying stop on the island; but all the boats sailed past it with little more than a nod, dropping anchor only at its more imposing neighbors— Schouwen-Duiveland, South Beveland, Walcheren.

There was news of government plans to close a part of the estuary. Perhaps there would then no longer be a North Beveland Island, or its configurations would be changed, and surely its life.

I had already begun to write about the village and its people—to preserve what I felt had been given to me in trust. But now I wanted also to write for the sake of the island itself; to record it as an island pummeled by the sea and reached only by boat. A place where true mariners lived, men with the rhythm of the tides in their blood and the distance of seas in their eyes.

~ Beth Merizon, Grand Rapids, Michigan

The Lay of the Land

In the broad estuary where the river Scheldt flows into the North Sea, the Zeeland islands for centuries lay watchful in the midst of a liquid turbulence. With the ebb tide the fresh water of the Scheldt surged out among the southern islands and mingled farther north with the waters coming down from the Waal and the Meuse. And later, when the tide turned, the salt seawater rushed in toward the riverbed, pressing with massive strength against the dikes and sweeping past the islands in a swift, formidable current. So it was at the time of this small history.

The islands are Schouwen-Duiveland, Tholen, St. Philipsland, North Beveland, South Beveland, and Walcheren. To the south lies Zeeland-Flanders, a part of the mainland bordering on Belgium, completing the area of the province.

North Beveland, in the very heart of Zeeland, lies like a part of a mosaic in the angle formed by Walcheren and South Beveland, its southern and western shores separated from them by the Zandkreek, at some points now hardly river wide, and the Veersche Gat, ranging from two to four miles in breadth. But to the north, northwest, and east the waters stretch far to the distant shores of Schouwen-Diuveland, Tholen, and St. Philipsland.

North Beveland bears little resemblance to the island under that name on medieval maps. Like the rest of the province, this small wafer of earth has again and again been overrun by the sea. Now this polder, now that, has gone down, and in the floods of 1530 and 1532 the entire island sank. It is said that sailors sailing up the estuary saw only the tips of the church steeples. Great numbers of inhabitants lost their lives, and for many years no effort was made to reclaim the land. Gradually new layers of clay accumulated on the old submerged fields and towns, and wherever these alluvial deposits were extensive and reached a sufficiently high level they were surrounded by low, temporary dikes. Later, as each reclamation became "ripe," higher, permanent dikes were constructed. Thus over a period of centuries, piece by piece, a new island was built, its polders deviating in size and shape from those of the old North Beveland.

If one were to fly over the island during the growing season one would see at a glance that it is a land of farming, orchards, and cattle raising. All blocked out in clearcut patches of green it would lie, with here and there rows and masses of bright colors where flowers bloom, and splotches of black or brown and white where herds graze in their pastures. Not a railway, not a tramway, defiles the land with its hard, metallic speedway; but bridges to the north and south now bring automobiles from outside in increasing numbers down the widened roads, and main highways bear signs and numbers to guide the tourists.

If in flying over you counted the sizable towns you would find one for each finger of your hand, besides a few small hamlets. Wissenkerke, Colijnsplaat, Kats, Kortgene, and Camperland—these are the five towns.

Colijnsplaat

When the disastrous flood of 1953 struck the islands, taking lives and destroying homes and farmlands, the Dutch government began searching for ways to protect Zeeland from the sea. As a result the great Delta Project took shape, an engineering feat comprising miles of seawalls, dams, and bridges. Built in the 1960s and 1970s, they now control the flow of water into and out of the estuary.

Colijnsplaat, lying close against the northern rim of North Beveland, changed with the changing estuary. Its harbor, formerly open to the North Sea and used mainly for commerce and transportation, is now a haven for pleasure craft as well, providing space for as many as five hundred sailboats. The modernized old Hotel de Patrijs entertains vacationers from near and far.

In the late nineteenth century when Jan and Jo were young, however, the long quay was like a protecting arm shielding the small harbor from rough seas. Here at flood tide the skippers' children watched for their fathers expected in from Rotterdam or Dordrecht, Antwerp or Flushing, while others waited to meet passengers off the ferry from Zierikzee. And retired seamen sat on the nearby wooden bench in their open shelter, visiting while gazing out to sea and keeping an eye on activities in the harbor.

On the main street, or *Voorstraat*, where the sturdy old houses stand shoulder to shoulder, a hack service provided transportation to the other towns—especially to Kortgene on the southern shore, where one could catch a ferry to South Beveland, and from there board a train, if one were really undertaking a journey, to the cities on the island of Walcheren—Middelburg, Arnemuiden, Flushing—or east to the mainland.

Colijnsplaat harbor

These two accomodations—the boats sailing out of the harbor and the hired carriages trotting off cross country—were the links between Colijnsplaat and the rest of the world. To many of the villagers the hack service was a luxury, to be indulged in only on festive occasions or for emergencies, and as casually as they walked to the Voorstraat they walked across the island for a social call or on business. A few families had their own horse and carriage.

But all in all, travel away from the village was slight; the little local shops, the school, and the churches satisfied the everyday needs of the people, and the habit of staying at home was strong. Around the edge of the town as if encircling it in a ring of security lay the orchards and the flat, fertile farms, whose milk and butter, wheat and potatoes, supplied the tables of the island folk; while on the north, fishing boats laden with seafood sailed in on the tides.

It was here at Colijnsplaat—on an island embraced by populous Europe but serenely removed from its traffic—that our family tree put down roots, spread its boughs, and bore its fruit in an era when neither wars nor floods devastated the land, and life went on in a tranquil rhythm of births, marriages, and deaths, Sabbath days and holidays, and the four unhurried seasons of the year.

Daffodils and Cuckoo Birds

A half mile east and south of the town, on a farm named High Meadow, a broad white house stood far back from the road. Its deep lawn was like a mingling of park and meadow, with an oval pool midway between house and road and just beyond the pool a row of trees that stood like a screen unfolded for privacy. Under the trees and beside the pool in springtime a great company of daffodils shimmered in the warming air. And when the daffodils left the daisies came—seas of them, white and pink and rosy red, rippling over the lawn and flecking the grass with color from the pool down to the roadside. This was my mother's early home.

As a blond, blue-eyed child, Jo with her brown-haired sisters used to stand among the daisies and call to the echo in the woods across the road, "Oo-hoo, oo-hoo," and then listen, enchanted, to the faraway elfin reply. There were cuckoo birds with their friendly call; and in the evening the song of the nightingales floated across the road to the windows of the rooms where the children lay drowsy in their beds.

Behind the house moved a more substantial world, where men worked in the fields and the barns from dawn to dusk. There might be eggs lying in the straw waiting to be gathered, or the dog treading the wheel that churned

Pails at well, sketch by Armand Merizon

the butter, or the milkmaid, her yoke laid aside, washing her pails and hanging them upside down on the rack in the sun. These were a few of the things that caught and held for a while the darting attention of the children. In the haying season they would run out over the stubble fields and ride in atop the high, precisely-stacked loads of hay; and when occasionally Johannes Liefbroer, their father's hired man, drove away on an errand they gleefully climbed into the wagon and jogged along behind Maatje, the dallying mare. Johannes was the gentlest of men, who could not use the whip without first giving a warning.

"Now, Maatje," he would say, "I'm going to have to give you a *klapje!*" And then the small blow would fall.

In the long afternoons of summer the children sometimes made a party of daisy petals, eating them from saucers with milk and sugar. If the day was especially warm their mother, Elizabeth, would call to them as they went out with their dishes and spoons, telling them to be sure to sit in the shade; but Jo never was able to appreciate this advice. The sunshine was so gay, so pleasant!

The farmhouse stretched to do double service in those early years, with Jan and Elizabeth De Jonge and their family occupying one side, while on the other lived Jan's brother Willem with his wife, Wilhelmina, and their children. Early winter evenings between supper and bedtime the young ones gathered in the long hall between the two apartments and rode the great rocking horse that had been made especially for them. It carried five or six children on its back, and its rockers were so long and graceful that as they dipped and rose they gave the small riders the illusion of flying out through space. Elizabeth sat near the stove those winter evenings, singing her youngest child to sleep, and as she sang she could hear from the hall the curved, rhythmic sound of the rockers and the musical voices of the children; while in the kitchen the maid watched the kettle of soup as it bubbled on the hearth for the hired help's supper at nine.

The time inevitably came when the house could no longer accommodate the two growing families. When Johannes, the fifth child, arrived to join his four sisters—Jannetje, Jo, Margrieta, and Prien—Jan De Jonge began looking for another place. Jo was just four when they left the farm, with its daffodils and pool and the echo across the way, to make their home in the village.

Jan remained a farmer and went out every day to work

on his land. In the open space behind his house at the edge of town he built a commodious barn; here he brought his cattle and horses after the long days in the fields, and here the children would come during harvest time to watch the threshers beat the grain with their flails.

Now instead of the fields and the deep, flowered lawn the children had the prim streets and their fenced-in yard for their playing ground. Jo was impressed and delighted with the one lilac bush in the village—blooming just behind the hedge that separated *Dominie* Van Leeuwen's parsonage from the street. Nearby in the same yard, its boughs extending out over the church moat, stood a medlar tree, whose small, pear-like fruit attracted after dark stealthy gangs of boys with ropes and long sticks and poles.

The restrictions of village life sometimes puzzled the wildlings so accustomed to the freedom of the countryside. There was a day when Jo and her older sister, Jannetje, cutting across a field on their return from an errand, were surprised to hear a woman shout at them for walking on her land. When she threatened to call the police they galloped home like terrified deer and burst into the room where Elizabeth sat knitting, her long checkered apron spread out like a tent around her. Under the apron they dove, confident that *Moeder* would not betray them. Slowly, as the minutes ticked away in the clock on the shelf and the dreaded knock on the door failed to materialize, the drumming in their hearts subsided; and finally, after what seemed to them a discreetly long wait, they crept out of the tent and explained their odd behavior.

A House that Faced the Dike

The village school stood like a guarded child between Dominie Van Leeuwen's house, with the lilac bush at its doorstep, and the spire-crowned church, which held the place of honor on the Doorspstraat, facing down the Voorstraat to the city hall and the harbor two blocks distant.

The broad Voorstraat was lined on both sides with linden trees that formed overhead two long green arcades. In the shade of the lindens lay bright, scrubbed sidewalks of golden-yellow brick. The houses, intermingling with the shops, extended out to the walks, their doorsteps swept and immaculate and their windows glittering in the sun and shade. Here lived *Mijnheer* Biebou the *burgomaster* and Mijnheer Vermeulen, the principal of the school; also Grastek, collector of internal revenue, and Dominie Schoolland, who could walk through his backyard to the Separatist Church on the next street west, the Achterweg. Marinus De Jonge, little Jo's uncle who operated the carriage service, had his home here, and Dr. Berkenfeld, the town's one physician.

The Voorstraat, sketch by Armand Merizon

At the north end of the street, on the east corner, stood the Hotel de Patrijs, its courtyard opening on the dike road and entered through an archway ornamented with a sandstone bear. Here the sound of the surf filled the air and the dike lifted its thick sloping wall, its vivid grass spangled in spring and summer with buttercups, white cowslips, and poppies. Many of the sea-going folk of Colijnsplaat lived in this part of the town, where the moods of the water drifted in and hung over the hem of the land. Our grandfather Adriaan Merizon, a skipper who ran a freighter to Rotterdam, lived in a square white brick house that faced the dike a short distance east of the harbor. Here my father was born, and here he lived the first nine years of his life.

From his bedroom window Jan could look out over the estuary and the North Sea, and on stormy days when the house shook with the pounding of the surf his window glass was wet with spray. At such times Jan's grandfather, Marinus Merizon, who was harbormaster, would patrol the dike with a corps of assistants, and there would be tension in the hearts of the men until the storm subsided. Sometimes when the Scheldt River water went racing out with the tide and the North Sea blew in with a gale, the two waters would meet in an impasse and rise in a high liquid wall. Then when the tide changed the sea would sweep in and beat with a double fury against the dikes.

Once when the sea was in this wild state our grandmother Lavina, a hearty, jolly woman, said suddenly to her little girls, "Look at that! Some day the sea will push that dike right in." Her words filled them for the moment with terror; but they looked at her bewildered, for after saying a thing as freighted with disaster she brushed their fear aside with her reassuring laugh and went about her work as though confident the dikes would stand forever.

Mostly Sea

There were no natural barriers to hold back the sea at any point along the margin of the island; it was entirely encircled by the outer dike. Inner dikes crisscrossed the land in seemingly haphazard lines and curves—tracing an artless record of the slow struggle to separate this small piece of earth from the sea, and providing protection to the individual polders in the event of a break in the outer dike. Towns and farms studded most of the polders; but the tides that in rough weather swept over the dike at the northwest section made that corner of the island unsafe for habitation. It was called the Unrest Polder. Men worked constantly there reinforcing the seawall. They wove large mats of saplings, weighted them with heavy stones, and lowered them from tugs into the seabed twenty-five to fifty yards out from shore. Other sections of the dike were constantly watched and also in frequent need of repair, especially the entire northern exposure, but the Unrest Polder required continuous care.

Looking out from the dike at Colijnsplaat one saw almost nothing but sea; to the north, to the west, and to the east the water stretched away to spacious distances. But Schouwen, the northernmost island in the Zeeland group, lay near enough to be a visible neighbor. Though to the north it was a good ten miles and more distant, to the northeast its coast curved down to a point only four miles from Colijnsplaat; and across this narrow stretch Adriaan Karreman plied his sailboat ferry, linking North Beveland with the ancient town of Zierikzee.

To the right, eastward, lay the island of Tholen, vaguely visible at times but too distant to be seen clearly, especially at ebb tide, when the fresh water sweeping round it wrapped it in a shawl of mist. The island seemed to come closer at night, when the beacon on its western shore penetrated the darkness.

Northwest and west of Colijnsplaat the North Sea waters stretched away illimitably. London lay almost due west—a hair's breadth south; and to the northwest, if one's vision could be extended indefinitely, one's eye would skim over the tip of Schouwen and follow the slanting eastern coast of Britain straight to the Orkney Islands and on past the Faëroes.

All the skippers' children were able to point out the location of the Banjaard Reef off the western shore of Schouwen. During the sixteenth and seventeenth centuries, when Veere in Walcheren and Brouwershaven in Schouwen were great shipping centers, and Holland was enjoying her Golden Age, the reef had come to be known as the sailors' graveyard—so many were the ships that foundered on its shallows. Its only virtue had been the protection it afforded the islands against the tremendous force of the flood tide; but under the constant movement of currents through years and centuries the great sand bar was wearing down, with the result that the pressure of the seas flowing in between Schouwen and North Beveland was increasing.

Another spot the children liked to search out when they went walking west on the dike was the Cream Pot (Roompot), an area in the water just south of the Banjaard Reef periodically churned into a mass of froth.

When the full light of day fell on the sea the skippers' daughters could gaze out toward the reef and the Roompot with a cool detachment; but sometimes they walked on the dike at twilight. Then the Cream Pot churning white in the gathering darkness and their thoughts of broken ships and drowning sailors sent chills down their spines, and they would shudder and turn and race back to the lighted streets of the village.

The Box of Gold

There were people who lived and died on the island without ever sailing the surrounding waters or setting foot on other soil. Skipper Adriaan once took an old gentleman to "the city" to visit his married daughter, and as they left the harbor behind and the island receded into the distance, he looked around with wonder on the far stretches of water and slowly shaking his head observed, "I never realized the world was so vast."

Often people came to see Adriaan about having packages shipped to the seaport city. One day a farmer knocked at the door holding in his hands a small, well-made box whose contents were apparently heavy. In the privacy of the closed-off living room he explained that the box contained a quantity of gold to pay off the balance of the mortgage on his farm. He wanted it taken to his bank in Rotterdam.

It was an unusual request, and of a more personal nature than most of the business that came under the skipper's care; but handling it as simply as another detail in the week's work he made out the necessary papers and, taking the box of gold, assured the owner that the transaction would be carried out according to instructions. It was clear from the farmer's whole bearing and his state of controlled anxiety that the matter was of great concern to him. Before he left he inquired when he could come for his receipt.

"We sail tomorrow with the midnight tide," Adriaan answered, "and we expect to be back in a week. You had better plan on Thursday."

The following morning the farmer was back. In shy embarassment he explained his second call. "My wife and I," he said, "lay awake all night, thinking, What if the boat should go down with our gold aboard!"

Adriaan hid his smile as well as he could and agreed that yes, there was always that possibility, but wasn't it rather remote? Then he suggested, "Why don't you take the gold to Rotterdam—take the train from South Beveland at Goes."

But the farmer shrank from the idea. "No, no," he demurred. "I would have to leave the island...."

And so, perplexed and helpless to find a safer way, he decided to leave arrangements as they were, and once more walked reluctantly away from the house where his gold, earned veritably by the sweat of his brow, lay waiting its voyage.

Pennies from Rotterdam

Through a small square window in the loft of the skipper's warehouse his flock of pigeons flew in and out all day long. Over them arched the wide sky of the lowlands; the grassy dike was their esplanade and the light-filled air over the estuary their flying space.

For the amusement of his two youngest sons, Adriaan occasionally took a pigeon on board when he left for Rotterdam, promising to release the bird at Dort (short form of Dordrecht) and telling them as nearly as he could the hour they could expect its return.

The boys would remember and scan the eastern sky. And when a dark point in the distant air gradually took on form and wings and continued toward them, it was as though they were receiving a personal salute from their voyaging father. Proud and gratified, they watched with increasing delight as the pigeon, coming nearer and nearer, finally tilted its wings, turned, and sailed in over its own threshold.

The skipper would be gone for a week at a time, and when the day of his expected return arrived Jan and Marinus would flip out of bed in the morning and run to the window to see if the *Lavina* lay in the harbor. If she did, they rushed into their clothes and sped down to the kitchen.

But if the familiar berth lay empty they would dress in a humdrum mood, reassuring themselves nevertheless that *Vader* would certainly come with the next tide.

At school the morning wore slowly away, its hours cut meticulously into periods for recitation and drills and laborious scratchings in notebooks. The harbor, the *Lavina*, and the route to Rotterdam were another world—crowded out of their thoughts by the master's many demands. But at last the noon hour came, and once outside they would run the length of the Voorstraat to the harbor and take a quick look. Perhaps the *Lavina* was already in; if she was, they would turn and race to the house; but if not, they kept going until they were out on the far side of the quay, scanning the water for the familiar brown sails or discovering them gliding in under their noses!

There was always something glamorous about the skipper during the first few hours of his return. Had he not been to the place where the great ships of the world met and docked? And had he not walked the streets of the immense city, visiting shops and banks and great commercial houses? The enchantment of the wide, hustling world lay upon him and drew the boys to him like a magnet.

But before they could go home with him and listen to the news, another matter awaited attention. The skipper always brought new pennies from the bank for the children, and as soon after the greetings as they could tactfully do so they would remind him, and he would reach into a pocket and drop into their palms the bright, diminutive copper coins. Then Marinus and Jan would race over to Sarah Vander Blouw's little store on the Achterstraat.

The store occupied a small front room in the house where Sarah lived. On shelves in the window facing the street she displayed pears from Spain, polished apples, molasses cones, and other sweets. Likely the boys would have to wait while another customer finished shopping. It might be a woman who had come with an empty cup to buy an ounce of sugar or a few peppermints, or perhaps it was a piece of American pork she wanted. Jan and Marinus would watch while Sarah weighed up the purchase on the balancing scales, using not the conventional brass weights with little knobs, like those of the merchants on the Voorstraat, but a set of stones in graduated sizes, worn dark and smooth from constant handling. Some had patches of tar added to bring them up to legal measurement; for once every year the government inspectors came and set up headquarters in the school building, and all merchants were required to bring their weights and measures and scales to be tested.

When the customer had her ounce of sugar or her piece of pork, or whatever she had come to buy from the small stock of staples, the boys would select their pears or molasses cones and lay their new coins on the counter. And Sarah, seeing how the pennies shone, knew that Skipper Merizon's boat was in from Rotterdam.

On Saturday

Saturday was a kind of special day in Colijnsplaat—a day for dressing up and savoring the joy of being alive. The streets and houses, bright and clean from their Friday scrubbing, appeared in the morning to have an air of expectancy about them. Here and there on the yellow walks of the Voorstraat groups of girls strolled with their knitting. Jan's sisters would be there, working with a will because they looked forward to an afternoon that would be all theirs, to spend as they pleased.

In the De Jonge home on the Achterstraat—the street just east of the main street—Jo washed the lamp chimneys and trimmed the wicks in an arched curve; and often, too, she helped her mother polish all the family's black leather shoes in preparation for Sunday. On fair, warm days they would work out in the yard behind the house, and as each pair was finished it was set down beside the others, until finally a long, black row stood twinkling in the sun.

But the afternoon was holiday, and when twelve o'clock

dinner was eaten Jo and her three sisters ran up the stairs and changed to their second-best, Saturday dresses. Over their dresses went clean starched pinafores; and into her pocket Jo would thrust a small rubber ball and her *pickelen*,[1] a game they would be playing sooner or later. So they would step out on a Saturday afternoon—Jo and her sisters, Jannetje, Margrieta, and Prien, and two cousins, Viena and Wilhelmina Potappel, who had walked in from just east of town where they lived in the house beside the mill.

A favorite stroll these holiday hours was the top of the dike, with its wide view of the water and its grassy slopes stretching brightly away for miles to east and west. If they were early enough they might see the ferry coming in on its daily run, bringing mail and passengers from Zierikzee and points beyond. Farther east they came upon the skipper's pigeons, waddling about, cooing, coasting through the air, and sometimes vanishing through the small opening high in the front wall of the warehouse.

Everything delighted the children on a spring or summer day—the movement of the birds, the flickering highlights on the water, the feel of the breeze that lifted their hair at the temples and pushed gently at their full skirts.

Over at Zierikzee the high windows of the medieval tower caught the sun and winked in its light, and Jo thought of how at sundown the panes in those distant windows turned a lovely crimson that filled her with delight. As the afternoon wore on the strollers would turn to their games, joining other children of the village in their Saturday play.

---

1 pickelen: a set of small knucklebones from a pig. They were set in different positions as the game proceeded. It was played something like jacks.

Zierikzee medieval tower

The town hall grounds were a magnet for the men on Saturday afternoon. Here they would gather to talk of shipping and commerce, of crops and the weather, or of national or international affairs. Skippers De Mul and Adriaan Merizon were in the habit of pacing back and forth, back and forth on the walk before the town hall, hands behind their backs, smoking their pipes and talking. Sometimes their small sons, Pieter and Jan, would take a notion to walk behind them, their hands clasped behind their backs, their short legs straining to keep stride with their fathers' long steps.

At three o'clock one of the clerks appeared in the doorway with a brass plate and a stick, and suddenly the air was shaken with a clanging sound. It was time for the weekly news. Many of the villagers subscribed to the *Zierikzeesche Nieuws-Bode* or to papers from Goes and Middelburg, and some read the *Rotterdamsche Courant*. But for local news—North Beveland news—they were dependent on the Saturday broadcast from the town hall.

At the sound of the clanging plate, men who had been standing around talking closed in to listen, while from their sheltered bench behind the hall the older men came hurrying to join them. Around the fringes of the audience children stood in twos and threes—not to hear what was being announced but to watch mischievously the faces and postures of the men as they listened. If something particularly exciting was reported the chewing and smoking was furious, and when the clerk had finished reading, out of pockets would come innumerable tinder boxes, and the smokers, standing now in little cliques, would strike their flints over their pipes and talk between their teeth.

While the men discussed the affairs of the day their wives at home donned fresh white caps and aprons and in anticipation of the coming Sabbath enjoyed a certain sense of repose. Their houses were swept and in order, the shoes were polished, the family's best clothes were ready for Sunday, and a supply of peppermints stood in a jar in the cupboard.

Lavina, Jan's mother, took the hammer and pounded a slab of *stokvis*—dried fish from Scotland hard as a stone—and hung it in the cistern, just above the water, to soften for the Sunday dinner. Soon it would be time for her sister Betje De Pree to come in from the farm with the butter, and they would have a cup of tea together. How quiet it was with everyone gone from the house! Maybe she could still finish those socks for Adriaan this afternoon. Taking her needles and yarn, she would go to the living room, where she had a view of the road along the foot of the dike. And as she sat knitting, the tick of the clock on the mantle was like a slow, measured obbligato to the staccato click of her needles.

The Potappel Mill

To return home after their Saturdays in the village, the De Jonge's small cousins Viena and Wilhelmina had only to walk out the Dorpstraat a little way into the country, where their house stood just to the left of the road. A driveway alongside the house led up a gently sloping incline to a swell of ground some distance back. There on a grassy plateau the windmill stood, rising like a beacon above the flat countryside.

The circular wall of the Old Mill, constructed of light grey brick, tapered inward toward the top, its smooth surface interrupted here and there to let in an arched window, and at the base three arched doorways. The heavy wooden doors and the panes of the windows were deeply recessed in the thick wall, and their unadorned apertures in the plain surface emphasized the simplicity and beauty of the old tower. Aloft, the four great wings turned with an easy but deliberate motion, as though however unbridled the wind at times might be, the mill would never surrender itself completely to wild excesses. High into the upper air the long wings swung their arc, then wheeled so low that even a cat could scarcely walk beneath.

Long before Josias Potappel came into possession of the mill, it had already been known as *De Ouden Molen*—The Old Mill—for it dated back to 1598. Another mill, built later, stood west of the village.

The Potappel's Old Mill

The wide house below faced toward town rather than the road, and each of the downstairs rooms—the kitchen, the living room, and the sitting room—had windows with a view toward Colijnsplaat. Before they reached home Viena and Wilhelmina, and sometimes Suzanna, would likely be seen by their mother or one of their older sisters. And by the time they stepped in at the door supper would be spread on the table.

One would not have thought, to see her, that their mother was a sister of Elizabeth De Jonge. Elizabeth was small, and younger by many years; Prien was large, and

Moe Prien Potappel

her many layers of clothes increased her appearance of amplitude. Ample she was in spirit, as well. Besides rearing her own twelve children she had made a home for her younger brothers and sisters at the time of her parents' death; and later, while most of her twelve were still with her, when Josias's brother died she took under her wing his three orphaned children—two girls and one boy.

Because of her wealth of experience the women in the neighborhood came to depend on Prien for advice and understanding. If a child fell ill—but not so ill that Dr. Berkenfeld had to be called—or if an appetite had mysteriously dwindled, the anxious mother would come and discuss symptoms and remedies with *Vrouw* Potappel over cups of steaming coffee. Likely there would be pastries, too, which Prien herself had made, for she was known for her cooking and baking. To the neighbors the house was regarded as a place of plenty, of easy openhandedness. They would say, "Dat is net een zoeten inval," a place where the sweets fall in.

Perhaps it was this spirit of ease and freedom that got into the bones of Bram's girl one summer day. Clouds were gathering and a wind was rising, and Bram, one of the miller's sons, was called to help a friend put in his hay. Quickly the girl slipped to the back of the house where his boots stood, and from a dipper filled the feet with water. That would keep him home! But to her surprise and dismay Bram did not seek her out and playfully accuse her. He strode off to help this neighbor, and he never asked to see her again.

Gerard and Bram and Willem—these were the names of the sons of the family. The other nine were girls. In no time at all—so the years had sped—Prien had daughters as tall as herself, and others in steps all the way down to Cornelia, who was in the first room in the village school. The three orphans of Josias's brother joined the family, and as time went on the boys became a quartet—Gerard and Bram, Willem and Bram *neef,* or nephew. They all learned to lend a hand among the wheels and hoists, bins and chutes and stones. And the white dust that is the mark of the miller came to settle as familiarly on their clothes as on their father's.

Josias had also his hired man, Bert—as skillful and at ease with the machinery of the mill as a sailor among the rigging of his boat. To the younger children of the family the mill might have been only another building on the grounds, a place where their father worked to earn their living, had it not been for Bert. His high-heartedness and a way he had of brushing everything with a sheen of humor lifted the winged tower above the realm of the commonplace. As far back as their young memories could go, Bert had been part of the very air and substance of the mill.

They loved to step into the dim interior and find him moving about amid the equipment on the milling floor. Over on one side the ground meal, coming down from the grinding floor above, would be flowing from a funnel into linen bags, while through another funnel, and from another pair of stones, flour poured into bins to await sifting. Nearby, the bolter turned to the tempo of the wings outside, separating the bran from the light-brown whole wheat flour.

Sometimes the children followed Bert up the stairs and watched the great stone discs revolve. The stones appeared enormous to them. They were wider across than even Bert could reach by stretching out both arms. One pair ground wheat into flour, the other crushed peas and barley and oats into meal for stock. If Bert went up to the third floor the young ones trailed along behind him. Here they saw the whole grain and the fodder hoisted up by a windlass from the ground level and fed slowly to the stones on the floor just below. But what attracted the children more than the movement of the machinery or the pouring of the grain was the thrill of looking out through the windows from this enthralling height. With their hands they would wipe an opening in the mill dust on the glass and then gaze out.

The neat, square fields of the island farms stretched away into the distance; and diminutive human figures, bending and rising at their work or traveling the earthen roads, took on a new significance in their wide, spacious setting. Looking to the north from one of the three windows the children could discover the sea and estuary. And perhaps while they gazed, every few seconds a long wing would slice through their range of vision, startling them in their reverie. From another window the sturdy tailbeam and its four braces, extending from the cap of the mill to the ground, were like giant bars between them and the outside world. The noise throughout the mill discouraged conversation, especially up here, for in the cap just overhead the wingshaft and the king cog labored to drive all the machinery in the mill. The stronger the wind, the greater the roar and rumble.

It was a joy to the children if while they were on the hoisting floor the position of the wings had to be changed. Running from window to window, they could peer down and watch the men outside move the tailbeam on its trundle wheel until the wings faced into the wind, and then secure it to one of the fence posts that encircled the tower.

About the only time the girls of the family were called out to help was in the event of a sudden high wind, when the mill would have quickly to be set neutral—the sails on the wings reeved and the wings set parallel to the wind. It was a tussle at times to bring the wings into position, and every sturdy arm was one more brace against those unimpeded winds of the lowlands.

There was another caprice of the weather that sometimes brought the older girls into the mill. If for days on end the air scarcely moved, or stirred only enough to toy gently with the sails, all the machinery in the mill would go to sleep and production would stop. But the bolter down on the milling floor could be turned by hand. So if a quantity of flour awaited shifting, Tannetje or Neeltje or one of their sisters would take the big wheel and turn it.

The hoisting floor was the limit of the children's explorations, for only the men went up into the cap—by ladder, when repairs or adjustments had to be made. And so after filling their eyes from each of the three windows they would be ready to clatter down. The rumble of the cogs in the cap gave way to the roar from the grinding floor, and as they looked down from the height of the steps the stones were like two giant tops, laborious in their spinning.

Then below them lay the milling floor, where in a

shaft of light a trillion specks of flour-dust floated on the air, and where Josias likely as not stood passing the time of day with a customer.

After the confines of the tower the air out under the sky was luminous and the lawn wide and free. In sheer joy of movement the children would run across the turf, hardly noticing the staid geese that waddled away at the sudden commotion.

Midafternoons Bert strolled over to the house in hope of some refreshment. He had his special little jokes with Prien. "Madam," he would say with a twinkle in his eye, "the mill windows are dusty again. Do you have a cup of brandy I could wash them with?"

"Hm," Prien would retort, "I think it would go down your throat before it touched the windows." And she would pour him a cup of tea.

The Green Cart

A little to the north of the Oude Molen a creek ran through the countryside. Its waters, flowing in and out with the tides and the opening and shutting of the sluice gates, were a blend of the currents of a great sea and a great river. But it was a common enough looking little stream, its borders lush with the growth of wild grasses and willows whose roots drank freely of its ebb and flow.

There were berry bushes, too, and on early summer days when island berries were swollen to ripeness Prien would send her children for a gathering of wild blackberries. They went out swinging pails and baskets, their hearts as light as the day was fair. The sun shone warmly on them as they worked, but with a gentleness that high latitudes can induce and the tempering vapors of a cold sea. Around them meadow birds fluttered and sang and rocked on swaying boughs, while the children wandered from bush to bush, always looking for the one most laden, the one with the plumpest and the ripest fruit. The berries grew large and would have filled the containers quickly had they not been so sweet to the tongue; but their sweetness prolonged the task.

When finally the children turned to go, their pails and baskets heavy with fruit, the mill tower marked their way, and the four great wings turning in the breeze were like a signal summoning them home.

There would be more than one such day during the short season, and Prien would put the berries down in a deep crock to turn slowly to wine. So she preserved against the bleakness of winter something of the warmth and sweetness of the summer sun, to be sipped appreciatively when harsh winds moaned about the house and buffeted the wings on the tower.

The house beside the mill was a familiar place to Elizabeth's children, especially to Jannetje and Jo. For the farm where they were born was out in this same neighborhood—around a bend in the road and out a way—and often in those early years when the family drove to town they would stop by and say hello to Prien and "Sias," and the DeJonge children would play a little while with their cousins.

Later, when they lived in Colijnsplaat, they spent whole days now and then at *Moe*[2] Prien's—long, delicious hours indoors and out, with meals that seemed like celebrations because so many came to the table.

Jo, sitting between Viena and Wilhelmina in the big family circle, would wonder how Moe Prien ever found time to satisfy her own hunger at her table, for she spread every slice of bread that was eaten by her brood. Tucking the big loaf under her arm she would slap butter or *stroopvet*[3] over the open end with a couple of broad strokes,

---
[2] Moe: Zeeland dialect for "aunt." Formal Dutch word is *tante*.
[3] stroopvet: A mixture of pork fat and syrup.

then slice the piece off, bringing the blade in toward her with deft, swift movements. Jo was always intrigued by Moe Prien's way with the bread.

After lunch when the children went out to play Moe Prien would call a warning to them. "Keep out of the way of the wings!" Her own hardly needed to be told. They had learned from the time they could walk to respect those long, swooping arms. But there was always a possibility... and besides, Elizabeth's children needed reminding.

Part of the mill's equipment was a two-wheeled green cart, used to carry flour and feed to the customers. When it stood outside the mill door the children knew that Bert was somewhere around. For where the cart went, Bert went. It was he who loaded the sacks in and pushed the cart off to town, or to the homes of the farmers who had brought their grain to be ground. His was a familiar figure on the Mill Path beside the road, and everywhere around he was known as Bert "van de Oude Molen."

On Saturdays if his load was not too great he often had two or three children in the cart among the bulging sacks. He carried a piece of old carpet along, so that when rain came he could spread it over the sacks and the children and go unworried on his way. At such times a passerby looking closely might have seen a pair or two of small hands holding up the edge of the covering, and wide blue eyes peering out in the wet world.

One morning when Jo's sister Margrieta was playing around the mill her cousin persuaded her to come along. Rain began to fall and the girls huddled under the carpet. Now and then, when Bert lifted out a sack and disappeared into a customer's house, they would push their covering aside for a breath of air. Rain and dust mingled freely on their hands and faces, and by the time they returned to the mill they were a comical sight—especially Margrieta, whose mussed-up hair accentuated the streaks on her face. Seeing her, Bert chuckled. He lifted her from the cart and carried her into the kitchen, where he held her before the mirror.

Poor Margrieta! One look in the glass and she was wild to be away. As soon as her toes touched the floor she was gone. Smiling and unperturbed, Bert returned to the cart in the drive and continued up the slow incline to the mill.

Viena's Birthday

Birthdays were almost commonplace in a family as large as the Potappels', but they did not go unnoticed, and sometimes there was even a party.

When Viena was ten years old her mother invited all the cousins over for hot chocolate and cookies. The house on the Achterstraat was high with anticipation as Elizabeth scrubbed and combed and dressed her four oldest children and sent them off bearing gifts.

Down the Achterstraat they went, then east on the Dorpstraat, away from the town and out into the country along the Mill Path. Jo had to curb her usual impulse to run and skip and dart off on little excursions, for she was taking to her cousin a cup and saucer of delicate china.

They assumed, on their arrival, that they would be taken into the living room on the left of the entrance hall, where they always sat when they went to Moe Prien's. But instead, when the door opened to their knock they were led into the room on the right—the guest-and-sitting room, which was used only on the rarest occasions. Here were chairs that were kept in the spit of polish week in and week out, and curtains so perfect one hardly dared breathe on them. The tall wardrobe shone resplendent, and there was even a cupboard bed, ruffled and curtained. But that was not strange; there were built-in beds all through the house—in the kitchen and living room and the small ante-room off the kitchen, where Bert slept, besides any number of bedsteads up on the second floor.

Bed cubby; origin unknown.

The little girls sat demurely in the polished chairs, speaking in subdued tones until gradually the feeling of formality subsided. But there was an elegance about the occasion that carried through to the end, to Jo's deep and half-conscious satisfaction. The flowered china, the little silver spoons, the cakes and cookies that were true party fare, and Viena, a little remote and shy and exalted....Jo was not one to sit still for any length of time, ordinarily; but there was something about the birthday reception in Moe Prien's sitting room that held her. She sat bemused, and only reluctantly did she rise to go when the circle began to break, and a guest here and there murmured, "Wij, moeten vertrekken." ("We must be going.")

The House on the Voorstraat

Back in the years before Marinus and Jan and Jaantje were born into the skipper's family, Adriaan and Lavina lived for many years in a house on the Voorstraat, next door to Mijnheer Biebou, the burgomaster. It was an everyday occurrence to see him step out in his silk top hat and Prince Albert coat and walk away on official business, carrying always his gold-headed cane.

Behind the curtained windows that reflected his passing figure, Lavina's living room sat in quiet decorum, its walnut and mahogany pieces aglow from their Saturday polishing. From the mantle over the hearth gleamed a pair of blue Chinese bowls; the secretaire seemed to be waiting for someone to sit down and pen a graceful letter in fine script; while the bland, closed fronts of the wardrobe and chest belied the array of intimate apparel that filled their deep interiors. A round table stood in the center of the room, and over near the doorway an arrangement of shelves called the spinne held choice dishes and the lacquered boxes and trays that had come halfway around the world from Japan. When guests came and tea or coffee was served the boxes were filled with cookies and passed around on their matching trays. Often in idle moments Neeltje and Leun would sit and study the decorations on the lacquered pieces and marvel at the Japanese ladies—their elaborate coiffures, their kimonos and fans.

Winter evenings, after the dishes were cleared away, the family gathered around the table in the living room, and Lavina and her two oldest daughters, Adriana and Elizabeth, would take up their sewing or mending. Across from them sat their grandmother Elizabeth Breas in her white cap and colored blouse, her hands just as busy as theirs; while beside her, one on each side, sat Neeltje and Leun, listening to the talk and taking turns threading their grandmother's needle. Sometimes after a session of sewing *Grootmoeder* would lay aside her work and reward the two small girls with a game of lotto.

Maria, the sixth child, was an infant when Adriaan found it necessary to trade the house for one of less value. And so it was that after some looking and considering they left their place on the Voorstraat for the square white house that faced the dike.

The only real disadvantage of the new home was its limited space. It provided no separate room for Grandmother Breas, whose helpful, benign presence had endeared her to every one of the children. She would be more comfortable now living with another daughter, Teune De Jonge-Breas. But that change hardly took her away after all, for from their kitchen door the children could look over to *Tante* Teune's backyard and see their grandmother on a nice day warming herself in the sun—so near did Teune and her husband David live. It was just around the corner and up the street a little way, near the house where they used to live.

A network of fences kept Neeltje and Leun from running through the yards to Tante Teune's. But they went constantly nevertheless, along the proper route—past the neighbors' houses and the sandstone bear that guarded the entrance to the hotel courtyard, then around the corner and a short run south. They had many a game of lotto with Grootmoeder, evenings, and Leun often spent the night with her.

Tante Teune's family was small, and the upper part of the house was unfinished except for one room. All the rest was attic. Leun soon learned, when she went up to sleep in that neat, immaculate room, to step into the attic to undress. Grootmoeder wanted no dust from the child's clothes sifting down onto her rug! But she said so kindly, if firmly, and Leun complied willingly for the privilege of spending the night as a guest. In the shadowy attic, on the edge of the soft splash of light that reached through the doorway from the lantern, she stood on the bare floor and changed to her long white gown.

She was always first to climb up and sink into the pool of feathers, and she lay very quietly, her dark head bright against the enormous white pillow, while Grootmoeder knelt a while beside the bed, and the clock on the dresser ticked loud in the otherwise silent room.

To Adriaan junior, the only boy in the family at the time of the move, the new location was infinitely better than the place on the Voorstraat. It was as near to the water as one could be and still live on dry land. From his window now he was able to scan the estuary for miles, and at night before getting into bed he could peer out and see the lights on the island of Schouwen, burning and flashing for whatever ships might be sailing those dark waters.

Homebodies

Those backyard fences were an expression of the desire for physical privacy, but they could be regarded also as a symbol of the reservations of the spirit. In a village so compact one could either become garrulous and lose his sense of his own identity or draw the lines carefully and observe the golden rule.

In Colijnsplaat the lines were drawn, and so habitual was their observance that for a woman especially one's house became one's world. When a girl married she almost literally went into her new home to stay. Her easy comings and goings were left behind with her girlhood, and she developed, perhaps, a shyness about being seen alone on the street.

When Lavina wanted to go to her sister Teune's, around the corner, she would send one of the children ahead to ask Teune to unlatch the gate at the far end of the lot so that she could go in through the back way, inconspicuously.

Leun and her sisters took this habit of their mother's

Girls visiting on the Voorstraat; origin unknown.

for granted, but they were perplexed over Teune's even greater withdrawal. The woman living directly across the street had been her close friend in their girlhood days. And now Tante Teune never skipped over there for a chat with her! Only on Friday mornings—when all the women were out scrubbing the walks, washing windows, and polishing the brass knockers—did they see one another, and of course on Sunday, when they went to church. When the *kermis* filled the Voorstraat with its splendid trappings Grootmoeder and Tante Teune were content to remain in the house and peer through the curtains once in a while. This the children could not understand.

As for walking through the streets to the store, a woman who had a child old enough to run errands would not readily go herself.

Perhaps the mirrors along the Voorstraat had something to do with this. To walk before a possible row of hidden spectators is not the most comfortable experience; and that was about what a stroll on the Voorstraat could be. For a woman sitting in her living room knitting or mending or visiting could through frequent glances at the mirror outside her window observe those who passed by.

All their pride and modesty, however, and all the force of habit could not keep the women at home when an invitation went out for afternoon tea. They would have braved a mile of mirrors to get together for one of those rare gatherings, when a *babelaar* on the tongue sweetened the tea and the bubbling conversation was enough to enliven the heart for many a day to come.

Ship Ahoy

On any summer evening that the *Lavina* lay in harbor at Colijnsplaat, the harbormaster or some sailor working on his boat might have seen a couple of boys come down to the quay at bedtime, jump onto the *Lavina's* deck, and disappear down the hatch. For Jan had a boundless enthusiasm for being on board, and he often persuaded his brother Marinus to come along and spend the night on the water.

There was something about sleeping on the boat that no bed on solid earth could give, and in their bunks in the forecastle they soon fell asleep to the sound of the lapping of waves against the prow, just a few inches from their ears. The best nights of all were those when a steady rain fell and thrummed on the deck overhead.

Skipper Adriaan had long looked forward to the time when his sons could sail with him; and as each of the boys grew old enough to take care of himself aboard he was allowed to accompany his father on one of the Rotterdam trips. By the time Jan became a seasoned voyager his brother Adriaan had finished school and was working regularly as shipmate on the boat. Marinus was not especially enamored of life on the water, but to Jan it was the best thing on earth. Once he had tasted the intoxication of days on board and felt the excitement of the seaport city there was no satisfying his longing to go again and again. He pestered the life out of his father.

But school attendance stood in the way, and summer vacations were of little help, since they lasted only two or three weeks. Happily, the skipper was aware that not all learning took place in school. He allowed his youngest son to come away now and then and make some discoveries of his own.

One day during the noon hour Jan was feeling especially bad about staying behind. Everything on land looked utterly stale; but the sea to the east—the route to Rotterdam—shone like a path of promise. He was out on the quay where he often stood when the *Lavina* was about to sail, and quite lost in his own thoughts when suddenly someone spoke. "Do you want to go too?"

Surprised, Jan looked up into the face of his Uncle Jan, who had strolled out to see the men off.

The foresail went up, fluttered, and bellied out, and the boat began to sail away from its berth. To Jan it seemed that his uncle was airing the question too late for any consequence, but he nodded, miserably. It was a simple matter for *Nom* Jan. He called and motioned to Adriaan to come close to the pier; and the next thing Jan knew, he was in the arms of Jaap Nieuwdorp, the deckhand.

The familiar smells of tar and rope mingling with salt sea air rose to meet him, and as he settled down to realize

Boys and boat at Colijnsplaat harbor; origin unknown.

the amazing and sudden change in his fortunes the movement of the boat through the water filled him with a deep contentment. He watched the island grow more and more distant, until finally it was compressed to so small a size that he could rest his eyes on the entire shoreline with a steady gaze. When the red roofs, the treetops, and the spires behind the dike had lost their identity and become part of a monotoned mass, he turned and watched the island of Tholen grow nearer and larger and more distinct, until finally its roofs and trees and towers came into focus.

The inland route took them directly east between the islands to the mouth of the Meuse, or Maas, up the winding river to Dort, and then north and west to Rotterdam. As they cruised along between Tholen and Schouwen and past St. Philipsland Jan became absorbed in the playful movements of the porpoises that swam with the *Lavina*, leaping through the air and diving into the bow wave, their smooth, supple backs brown and sleek and shining in the wetness. And all the while, as the water lifted and fell and slid past the gunwales, the thought of the six flawless days that lay ahead made perfect every small pleasure.

Leaving St. Philipsland behind, they came out into the Krammer, the broad mouth of the Meuse. Here Jan always went forward and watched with anticipation, for very soon now they would be meeting the side-wheel steamer to Zierikzee. On his first trip his father had presented the steamer to him as a surprise. He had sent the boy down to the galley to help Adriaan prepare supper, and told the deckhand to close the hatch. Then when the steamer was in full view and very near, he ordered the hatch opened and called Jan up.

It was a stunning moment. The big black hull and grey superstructure were imposing beyond words, and the red funnel spouting thick black smoke was simply stupendous. From that moment, Jan's ambition was to own just such a steamer.

It kicked up a heavy wash, and Adriaan cut close by so that the boys could feel the spray, smiling with pleasure himself at the commotion the bigger boat left in its wake. He was a man perfectly built for his role as skipper—compact, quick, and lithe. Everything he did on board was done with ease and dispatch. He wore the brown costume of the North Beveland seaman and a cap of black cotton—an inexpensive kind that had grown popular with sailing men because so often their headgear was whipped away by the wind. When rain fell he exchanged the visored cap for a sou'wester and trusted his smooth brown wool to shed whatever drops pelted it.

From the Krammer they entered the Volkerak, the passage that flows between Overflakkee and North Brabant, and then swung east into the Hollandsch Diep, where the strong currents of the Waal and the Meuse had cut an area unusually deep and difficult to navigate. It required the crew's full attention to take the *Lavina* up this stretch and safely into the Dordsche Kil, a narrow branch of the Meuse leading north to the city of Dort.

Throughout the voyage their view of the land on either side was cut off by grassy dikes; but magenta roofs and treetops in rows, and here and there a spire or the revolving wings of a mill gave evidence of human activity close by.

The sharp sea air and the continuous motion of the boat filled Jan with drowsiness long before dark. Soon after they had passed the steamer he went below and crawled into his bunk, where the slush-slush of the bow wave put him to sleep almost instantly. But he slept with one ear cocked, so that on their arrival at the Werme Quay in the Dort Roadstead the clatter of the anchor chain directly overhead would wake him. Hearing that metallic clank he tumbled out and dressed and hurried up the brass-tipped steps to the deck. He had to see the lights of the river traffic and especially the long railroad bridge at Moerdyk, which they had passed a short distance back. His father had told him it was one of the longest bridges in the world—it spanned a mile and a half of sprawling river waters—and he wouldn't have missed it for anything. Besides, it was something to report back to Colijnsplaat, where an audience always waited to hear what he had to tell. If a train passed over the bridge before he went back to his bunk the day was complete, utterly.

Next morning, while the chimes in the old Spanish church tower filled the air with their quarter-hourly music, the skipper started out for the offices of the shipping

Railway bridge at Moerdyk. 1882 wood engraving.

brokers; and with him went Jan, wearing his short jacket and knee-length black pants and a small black cap that covered the crown of his dark hair. It was something to be here with his father, in a city where traffic stopped by from all directions and great distances. Everyone came to Dort sooner or later, it seemed, and the variety of boats in the harbor and of costumes on the streets was enough to keep one's eyes busy all day.

When business calls were completed Adriaan would sometimes take the boys for walks away from the docks, where the quiet water of the canals mirrored rows of thick-crowned trees and fine old houses, whose upside-down versions were a permanent back-drop for the reflections of people walking by or crossing bridges, or moving about on the decks of their slowly-gliding boats.

After a day or two, depending on the amount of cargo to be transferred, they left the tree-lined embankments of Dort and headed for Rotterdam, sailing down the Noord River, a branch of the Meuse, to where it met the Lek and later the Yssel and then flowed on in broad grandeur as the Nieuwe Maas. There was not a dull stretch all the way. Barges, tugs, fishing boats, steamers—craft of all kinds—thronged the rivers; and the trees and houses that dotted the shores gave way, as the travelers neared Rotterdam, to industrial plants, shipyards, and factories, until the river banks became a veritable hive of activity.

Skillfully they maneuvered toward their port of destination, the skipper and his crew going about their business while Jan took in every detail of the shifting scene.

At last only a drawbridge separated them from their berth in the harbor. As they approached it Adriaan blew his whistle, and immediately from up in his tower the bridge keeper swung a tin cup, dangling from a line and pole, square in front of the skipper at the helm. Jan stood close beside him, all prepared for this moment. He reached up and dropped in the dime, the *dubbeltje*. Then the cup soared away and the bridge slowly parted. It was as though the world were bowing to their needs.

In Rotterdam

They berthed in the Haringvliet Quay, near the big naval training ship—a full-rigged, three-masted vessel that had originally been an East India frigate.

From this blissful anchorage, which seemed to him like the very hub of the world, Jan went on excursions into the city with his father and on thoroughly satisfying walks with his brother along the great stretches of waterfront. Wherever they went, they went on foot. The only alternative would have been the steam trams, but they were exasperatingly slow. As the trams lumbered through the streets they were heralded each by a man with a bell; all day the bellmen walked ahead, ringing a warning to pedestrians and clearing the way for the great mechanical monsters.

As the skipper and his son stepped along Adriaan would call the boy's attention to the statues of national heroes and tell him something of the lives and achievements of these men. But impressed though Jan was, and ready to give all the respect due them, he was far more intrigued by the two pairs of sandstone lions that guarded the approaches to the Koningsbrug, or Royal Bridge, which linked the old city with the broad streets of the new.

The network of rivers and canals made the city one with the sea, its low skyline constantly changing as sails and stacks slid by in their unhurried way. Jackknife bridges rose and fell, and swinging bridges parted unbelievably.

Especially good were the hours when the skipper, meeting other sailing men of his acquaintance, would sit down with them at some sidewalk cafe for a glass of brandywine. Half listening to their talk and absorbing the scene around him, Jan would wait without impatience. When his father's glass was almost empty it would be given to him, and he would have the wine-soaked sugar that lay undissolved at the bottom.

On Sunday mornings, when the sound of the water slapping the boats was more noticeable than usual in the quiet air, Jan went up on deck early to watch the boys from the training ship leave for church. Some, he had been told, were no more than twelve years old. After pouring out of the ship like a swarm of bees from their hive, the trainees formed lines four abreast and marched away. In their dress uniforms of white blouse, white cap, and navy blue pants they made a striking picture, and their weekly parade was one of the highlights of Jan's visits to the seaport city.

Jan, too, would be in dress clothes—except for the time he sailed unexpectedly—and soon he and his father, Adriaan, and Jaap would leave for Dominie Klinker's church. Lavina was careful to see to it when they left home that her husband's navy blues and the boys' black dress suits went aboard, along with the accessories that completed their Sunday dress. When the four walked down the aisle and into the pew no one would have guessed that they had just stepped off a small freighter in the Haringvliet.

For Jan, the pipe organ in the city church was a source of entertainment. Besides the music itself, rolling and swelling and receding into the distance, there was the curious sight of the man who did the pumping, rising and bending at the lever beside the organ. Of course, the *Groote Kerk* in Colijnsplaat had an organ; but a member of the Separatist Church did not readily visit there. It was good that here in Rotterdam they could come and go as they pleased, with no one paying the slightest attention.

They returned to the boat for their dinner, and the skipper doffed his coat for a turn in the galley; but by two o'clock he and his sons were back in the pews for the afternoon service. Sunday evenings he often invited acquaintances to join him on his deck, where they would sit on canvas folding stools and smoke and discuss the sermons they had heard that day, or other theological matters. Jan, sitting nearby in some inconspicuous spot and thinking his own thoughts, grew sleepy under the syllables of heavy talk, and long before the late northern twilight ended he would call it a day and go down to his bunk.

Although all of Rotterdam was a happy touring ground for Adriaan and Jan, no other part could compete with the American and East Indies docks. Here the air was so charged with the glamour and endless possibilities of far-off places that it filled the boys with excitement and longing.

There was, for example, the passenger steamer from the Indies. With its buff railings and awnings and its white topwork it possessed a cool, fresh, airy appearance that suggested the warm climate of the tropics.

There were full-rigged, three-masted freighters, too,

out of whose holds mysterious looking Malayans rolled bales and hogsheads of spices that filled the air with new and strange aromas.

The American docks had not the mystery, the strangeness that the ships from the Indies gave to their quays. Here was something thrilling in its bigness and splendor, but also more familiar and probable. The sight of the Holland-America ships awakened in Adriaan and Jan half-conscious dreams that had at times been tentatively transformed into hopes. For at home they often heard talk of going to America; and now here before their very eyes were the ships that had been there and were going again.

One day as Adriaan, Jan, and Jaap strolled along the Holland-America piers they stopped to linger beside the SS *W.A. Scholten*. Something about the ship appealed to them strongly, and they went over it again and again with approving eyes. Perhaps it was the grace and sweep of her lines that entranced them, together with the wonderful array of masts and yards and furled sails. There were stacks, too, rising in the midst of the rigging—big black cylinders picked out jauntily in green and white. As they discussed at length the ship's features and made their happy observations Adriaan discovered the sailing flag flying at the foremast. "She is ready to sail!" he announced, with all the authority of experience. "She will go out with the next tide."

They longed to watch the ship depart, but it would be hours til then, and they knew their skipper would not allow them out until midnight. Little did they surmise, when finally they started back to their boat, what untoward fate awaited the *Scholten* just over the western horizon.

During the harvest season Adriaan brought the samples of grain from the island to the brokers in Rotterdam, each small quantity of kernels in a white canvas drawstring bag, called a monster, with the skipper's name stamped in ink and a ticket attached giving the name of the farmer. At the brokers, samples from near and far were set out on tables, the tops of the bags rolled back so that the grain lay exposed for buyers to examine and compare.

Adriaan sometimes had to hurry back to North Beveland by train or the Zierikzee steamer to notify the farmers of their orders, leaving the shipmate and the deckhand to take care of unfinished business and bring back the boat. Then on his next trip he would haul the grain to the city. Jan never managed to have a part in one of those quick return trips with his father. His steamer ride, could he have known, was to come eventually, but under what different circumstances!

On their arrival back in Colijnsplaat after having seen the *Scholten*, Adriaan and Jan heard from their mother a story that stunned them with dismay. The ship they had so admired, the one they had seen with sailing flag flying and in readiness to depart, had been rammed in two in a fog in the English Channel, by the British steamship *Rosa Mary*. It was said that most on board had gone down.

SS W.A. Scholten

Jan hearing the news went off by himself to blink back his tears. She had been such a beautiful ship, such a very beautiful ship. He saw again, vividly, the clipper hull with masts and yards and sails, and the stacks that indicated her steam power—big, handsome black stacks banded in green, and the green bordered narrowly in white.

It seemed too much that that ship, the finest, he was sure, of all Rotterdam, should now lie broken and still at the bottom of the sea.

School Days

Drie maal een is drie.
Drie maal twee is zes.
Drie maal drie is negen.
     —from the Table of Threes

On school days in warm weather the lines of the multiplication tables floated out on the air in a singsong chorus of childish voices, and villagers walking along the treelined Dorpstraat listened to the droning with satisfaction. Their fathers and mothers before them had been quick at figures, and it was a matter of pride with them that they and their children after them should do as well.

Like the church that stood beside it, the school was of white brick, aged and weathered and grey. A long, narrow building, it would have appeared quite insignificant were it not for the tower that held aloft the one bell in the town. The school bell was the only voice that could reach the community for miles around, and its tone seemed to vary with its message. When it called the children to school it was cheerful, preemptory. It tolled mournfully during funeral processions; and once in a long while, when an emergency arose, it clanged with a wild urgency, sending a note of alarm over the countryside. When the dike that protected the polder west of the village sank, the school bell summoned all the men within hearing to hasten and throw up a barrier against the sea.

The entrance to the school was recessed within a dim, cavelike vestibule under the tower; and the door opened directly into the first classroom. Here the beginners sat on their long, low benches. Near the west wall at the farther side double doors opened into the second room, and similar doorways beyond led into the third and fourth rooms. Through these openings the school children thronged four times a day, while the teachers used other doors along the east wall, conveniently near to their desks. All was airy and spacious, with broad, high windows bringing in a flood of light.

On the left was the rectory of the Reverend, next was the entrance to the public school, and to the right was the tower of the Dutch Reformed Church. Origin unknown.

When Jo entered the school for her first day, wearing proudly on her left arm the marks of her vaccination, she was surprised to have Mijnheer Mouton pass out sheets of comic pictures in full color. She had expected to be put to work immediately on some impressive assignment, and this unexpected touch of brightness and humor delighted her. But the following day was all lessons, and before long the children were deep in *lezen, schrijven, rekenen, and spellen* (reading, writing, arithmetic, and spelling). Life took on a new importance, and now besides her ball and pickelen and her starched handkerchief, Jo carried in her sack under the slit in her dress her *potlood* and *griffel*—her pencil and slate pencil. And she began to use more freely the Dutch language, which in its pure form she had heretofore heard only in church; for at home and in all her play she heard and spoke the Zeeland dialect. It was bewildering at first, this having to juggle two languages and to keep them in their proper places. If she used the word "moe" at school her teacher would remind her to say "tante"; but if, forgetting where she was, she greeted her aunts as "Tante Viena" or "Tante Prien" she would be suspected of putting on airs. Gradually she learned to watch her quick, spontaneous speech and to keep her dialect out of the schoolroom, but to use it faithfully everywhere else—except in Sunday School, of course, and catechism class.

Like the beginners, the children in the second room sat on benches without backs, their desks long slanted boards with a shelf underneath for books, slates, and paper. It seemed the boys were expected to grow suddenly like weeds when they came into this room, for the rear benches where they sat were built so high that their feet dangled in the air. Jan quickly learned to lay one hand on his desk, one on the bench, and swing himself up into place. His *klompen* he left below. There were wooden shoes in twos all along the tile floor, their owners' feet in hand-knitted woolens swinging above them. In winter many of the klompen were lined with straw, or with pads of wool or carpeting.

Above the wainscoting the rooms were separated by a clear glass wall. From their new elevation the boys could look down on the first and second graders and feel that they had come quite a way. They began to study geography—*sardrijkskunde,* or earth-kingdom science—with colored maps unrolled on the wall and Mijnheer Vrulst doing his best to make the immense world real to the small islanders.

During history class the map of Europe hung unfurled while the children were taken far into the past. They heard tales of wars and sieges and humiliating periods of subjection to foreign powers; and to Jo the word Spaniard, pronounced with singular force in the Dutch language, came to have a frightening and sinister sound. When now the children sang "Wilhelmus van Nassauwe" and "Wien Ne'erlands Bloed" the songs had new meaning for them. They filled the room with their melodies, though there were boys who thought all this singing absurd and held themselves aloof from such emotional outbursts.

The map of Europe was furled, and another, a close-up of Holland, came down. The pointer rested on the city of Leyden, and the story of the siege was told. And who, they were asked, came to the rescue of those brave, starving people? Eight hundred Zeelanders! They sailed over the inundated land, fought the Spaniards among the spires and treetops, and entered the canal leading into the city, bringing with them food and freedom and victory. The teacher appealed to provincial pride again and again. He reminded the children that Admiral Michel de Ruyter, "the greatest admiral of his age," was a native of Flushing, over on the island of Walcheren. And of course they all knew Jacob Cats, the beloved writer and statesman whose verses were familiar to all Holland. "Father

Cats," he was affectionately called. He had been born in Brouwershaven. Surely they had all seen from the dike on a clear night the great beacon at Brouwershaven? And it was in Zierikzee, their neighbor city across the Ooster Scheldt, that Jacob Cats went as a boy to Latin school.

All day the children sat in their uncomfortable seats, hardly aware of their discomfort but restless with a need for activity. There were sewing lessons for the girls, but they were poor relief from book work, and Jo sometimes found herself still in her seat after school, paying the price for talking.

"Ik moet mijnzelf goet gedragen," she wrote, covering her slate with line after line. "I must conduct myself well."

The boys did not always get off so easily; they were sometimes flogged, and for some small misdemeanor they spent blank periods standing in the corner, face to the wall. On one occasion when he had gone to Rotterdam without notifying his teacher, Jan was told on his first day back to stay after school and take his place in the corner. It was a wretched feeling, standing there while everyone else hurried out to the sweet freedom of the fields and the dike. Suddenly as the upper classmen filed through the room on their way out one of them, Jan's cousin Adriaan De Pree, left the line and walked along the glass partition to where Jan stood. "Come along," he said, tapping the boy on the arm. Jan followed without hesitation, sensing in the tall fellow a certain authority.

As they approached the door Adriaan wagged a warning finger at the astonished teacher, and out they strode, like two princes passing the palace guard.

"Plaatjes! Gornet!"

Early in the spring of the year a familiar and welcome cry sounded in the streets. "Schordein bij de haven!" or "Gornet bij de haven!" And the boy calling out would ring his bell with a will to make sure the housewives heard his call.

The women went to their cupboards for a dish or a basin and stepped out into the street, their hearts cheered at the thought of the fish dinner they would be able to prepare. In no time at all the village was alive with women walking down to the harbor for a few scoops of sardines or shrimp, or whatever the catch happened to be.

The small May herring, or sardines, were delicious and sweet when fried, and a good generous scoopful could be had for a dime. When the skipper was home between trips to Rotterdam he often fried the fish for Lavina. He had learned long ago, in the galley of his father's boat, how to fry a spiderful of sardines to a golden perfection. He laid the little fish close together in the pan, their tails at center and their head ends radiating out like the spokes of a wheel. When they were delicately browned on one side he would turn the whole mass over in one piece. Neeltje and Leun and Maria often stood by and watched, their mouths watering as the scent of the crisping fish rose and spread through the kitchen. The salt sea air that blew over the island gave all the children appetites, and they ate readily whatever good, simple food was set before them.

Often at dinnertime Lavina covered a plateful of the hot sardines with a napkin and sent Jan running down the road to the home of a laborer's family nearby. Many men who worked by the day on nearby farms received such a pittance that they could hardly afford to buy a little fat for frying fish.

Mossels, or clams, grew out on the reef, and many islanders went out during low tide to gather a panful for a meal. They could also buy them from the fishermen at the harbor. After the clams were boiled and shelled they were served with melted butter or hot butter gravy and freshly-grated nutmeg, topped with a golden sprinkling of crushed rusk.

A curiously shaped fish also gathered on the reef was the sea snail, or *kreukel.* Boiled in salted water, these were brought to the table in their shells and eaten with long pins. The children especially enjoyed eating them. The little scale-like cap over the opening had first to be removed; then the fish was plucked out and eaten whole. Kreukels had a peppery taste; they were delicious and hearty eaten with bread and butter, and when the family left the table their plates were well covered with the little hollow, curled shells.

Now and then the village women could buy seafood at their door, from Job the fishman. He had his own small boat and peddled his catch in many a Zeeland village. Carrying his wares in two enormous baskets that swung from a yoke on his shoulders, he strode through the streets crying "Plaatjes! Plaatjes!" if he had sole, and flounder; or "Gornet!" if it was shrimp he was selling that day. He wore a blue wool shirt with a red bandana tied round his throat, a brown pea-jacket with trousers to match, and a cap with a stubby visor.

Elizabeth, hearing Job's call, would take her large white potato dish and her coin purse and step out at the front door. If the children were anywhere near they came running and sat on the doorstep to watch the transaction, for although Job was a familiar figure he somehow remained a curiosity. Curly sideburns burgeoned out from his temples and down along his jaw to his untrimmed beard, wreathing his oily face in hair. And the fishy smell that clung to his clothing enveloped him like an aura.

He would lay a mess of sole or shrimp on the overturned cover of one of the baskets and state his price. "Vijf en twintig cent," or "vijf en dertig cent." Then at Elizabeth's nod the fish were transferred to the white dish, and she would pay him and turn and go back into the house, her long full skirts trailing up over the doorstep behind her. And Job, again calling out, would continue down the street, where other doors were swinging open and women in white caps waited, a dish in one hand, a coin purse in the other.

There would be seafood on many tables in Colijnsplaat, come the dinner hour.

Zee Kraal

The seabed off Colijnsplaat lay level as a table top for a quarter of a mile out. There on the reef the *zee kraal* grew in scattered patches, its straight, tender shoots rising four or five inches above the sand. It was a tasty vegetable when cooked and eaten with potatoes and fish or meat, and it was a delicacy eaten raw.

The plants were inaccessible most of the time. Living and growing under the water, they stood uncovered and exposed for only a few moments twice a day—at six o'clock in the morning and again at six in the evening. Now and then a venturesome villager would hurry out and snatch a few of the stalks.

The sons of the skippers made a sport of going after the kraal. In their wooden shoes they would fly out over the hardpacked reef, its surface carved in parallel ridges by the receding waves, and leave a trail of broad footprints behind them. They went ostensibly to gather kraal, either for themselves or as a special treat for their mothers or a grandmother or some other favored person who was especially fond of the delicacy. But what really attracted them more was the urgency with which they had to work, and the excitement of having to evade danger.

The plants were like young bamboo or asparagus shoots—pointed at the tip and jointed along the shaft. Using his curved forefinger and the end of his thumb, Jan would nip the stems off at their base and quickly tip each shoot upside down before transferring it to his left hand; for they were filled with a juice that gave them their unique flavor.

The boys hardly had time to gather a good fistful; no sooner had the water subsided, it seemed, than the foaming edge of the incoming tide tumbled toward them and they had to run for their lives. Out at the edge of the reef the seabed dropped suddenly to a depth of four to five hundred feet. Schouwen had a similar reef extending south toward North Beveland, and when the in-rushing tide lifted the water in the deep channel between the islands, the spillover onto the reefs poured in with a suddenness that could be deadly to anyone out on foot and unwary. One evening Jan did get caught as he was running toward land. The water licked his feet, reached his ankles, and then surged around his legs. Without help he would have been lost. But Adriaan his big cousin turned back to pull him out and dragged him just ahead of the tide all the way back to the dike.

The kraal did not grow lavishly, and the difficulty of gathering the little there was kept it in high regard among the villagers. The boys felt they were making a real gesture when they offered their fistful to a favored one. Jan often took his small harvest to his Grandmother Merizon, over on the Achterstraat. "Bomma" was fond of the kraal, and this was one way he had of thanking her for the pennies she so generously gave him during kermis week.

There were island men who made a business of gathering zee kraal and peddling it through the villages. From them the housewives could buy enough to prepare as a vegetable for the table. They stewed it gently and served it with melted butter and nutmeg.

Whenever Elizabeth De Jonge bought kraal from the peddler her brood clustered around her and begged for a shoot to eat raw. There was something tantalizing about kraal—an elusive quality quite unlike anything found in other foods that made eating it a delightful experience. The cell walls in the plant are exceptionally thin and fragile, and the stalk seems to have no fibrous texture. Little Jo noticed how when she took a bite there seemed to occur in her mouth a delicate explosion of air and juices, and then the whole substance, full of tang, melted away. The shoot had something of the taste of spinach about it, and something of rhubarb; but it was different from either of these.

The word kraal also means beads—*kralen*. Perhaps in the far past some imaginative lover of words observed that the plant with its stem of many sections resembled a row of beads on a string, and so gave it that descriptive name.

Zee kraal in low tide.

Spoon Food

On the simply spread tables of Colijnsplaat eggs were as rare as fish was common. Not that they were scarce in that locality; all the farms encircling the village produced them. But the great city markets were able to outbid the frugal pocketbooks of the village housewives.

And so when Easter Sunday came and the families feasted on eggs, they were regarded by the children as a treat—a special holiday delicacy.

In the house that faced the dike, on Easter morning, the uncooked eggs were laid on the kitchen table, and the children were allowed to choose their own. When Adriaan was still young enough to care he was given first choice because he was the first son; the others followed according to age, while the two oldest sisters, Adriana and Elizabeth, looked on from the heights of their maturity. Each wrote his name on his egg; then Lavina placed them in a fishnet bag and lowered them into the kettle.

At the De Jonges', too, there would be eggs for breakfast

and dinner. Jannetje and Jo, Margrieta and Prien, stood around the stove to watch their mother lift the hot, dripping bag from the steaming water.

Whenever another child was born to Elizabeth her trays included eggs that had been bought especially for her. To Jo there was something festive about eating from a tray, and she often kept her mother company while she enjoyed her meal. There was an attitude of expectancy about the little girl as she sat beside the bed, and Elizabeth understood. She knew where the child's treasure lay. She would lift the little severed head from the egg in the egg cup and give it to her.

Sometimes it was Jannetje who received the treat, or Margrieta, or one of the other children.

Let a birthday roll around and the De Jonge kitchen was fragrant with the wheaty aroma of pancakes. For these special days Elizabeth made big ones that almost covered the plates. The children would choose between sprinkling them with sugar and rolling them or eating them with syrup.

In their lessons at school pancakes became *pannekoeken*, but at home they were *plattekoeken*, or flat cakes.

Many meals eaten by the islanders were as simple as a warm meal could possibly be. Supper might be a great kettle of soup or porridge—nothing else. There would be enough so that the plates could be filled again and again. Sometimes it was *pallegastepap*, or barley gruel. And again, *karrepap*—oatmeal cooked in buttermilk. Rice, fluffy and white, was often a meal by itself; and also wheat cereal cooked with milk for a porridge called *bree*, or a prune porridge—*pruime moes*. Whatever the hot plateful was, it would be sweetened with thick black syrup. Letting the dark stream fall from the big spoon to their plates, Jannetje and Jo made designs and letters and pictures, trying to outdo each other in stunning effects.

All these one-dish meals were known as *lepelkost,* or spoon food. During the half hour before the meal was served some hungry child might ask Elizabeth or the hired girl, "What are we going to have tonight?" And then the word would go around. "Wij hebbe lepelkost van avend." ("We're having spoon food tonight.")

At Whitsuntide

At *Whitsuntide* the streets of Colijnsplaat were lively and colorful with crowds of holiday-makers. After the spiritual observance of Pentecost in the churches on Sunday, a festival of joy followed on Monday and Tuesday.

In the Voorstraat under the high lindens girls and young women jumped rope until they were ready to drop. All up and down the street one could see the heavy ropes whirling in arcs over the bobbing white-capped heads, and hear the shuffle of feet and the slap of the ropes as they struck the pavement. A girl running in had to time her entrance just right, and once in she had to jump fast; for there were two ropes whirling in opposite directions, one swinging down and in, while the other swept out and up.

The young men from the farms had groomed their horses with loving care. In smart black breeches they rode them bareback or walked beside them through the town. The braided manes and tails of their steeds were intertwined with brilliant flowers—peonies, sweet william, and flaming poppies that could have been plucked from the landward side of the dike. Some of the manes had been braided hours ahead of time and then combed out to fall in waves with flowers fastened close to the head on each side.

There came an hour in the day when the rope jumping and all other activities in the town ceased, and the villagers and farmers strolled out along the road that led to the Old Mill. There the young men put on their traditional ring-riders stunt. A trellis that had been built to arch the road was tufted with a bright matting of fresh flowers. From the arch, and loosely attached, hung a row of rings suspended on cord.

As the time for the stunt drew near the villagers and the farmers stood waiting in the mill path and along the roadside. Presently the riders rounded a gentle curve and cantered into view. One by one they approached the arch and hurled their wooden lances, aiming at one of the rings. The spectators watched intently, and whenever a ring was carried away on a lance a great cheer went up while hands waved in the air.

To the children in the crowd the riders were splendid and their stunt was something to see, but the horses were the greater attraction. There was something of pageantry in those spirited, flower-decked steeds. Jan noticed how the red poppies stood out with startling brightness against the mane of an occasional grey horse.

Between the mill road where the riders passed and the mill path where many of the spectators stood, a narrow creek flowed out to the sea. Little Jo with her brother and sisters had managed on one such day to find standing room along the edge of the path facing the road; only the creek lay between them and the riders. Jo became so absorbed in watching that she forgot to brace herself against the pressure of the crowd; and suddenly, without warning, she found herself in the creek. She was out in no time, her clothes sticking to her skin and her nice leather shoes squishy with water. As fast as she could she slithered through the crowd, followed by a little band of faithful ones.

When they reached home her mother hurried her into dry clothes and her wooden shoes; then she set all her excited brood around the table and served them bowls of hot prune porridge, made with milk.

A Box to Own

In the evening, just before dusk, the lamplighter walked through the streets, a supply of matches in his pocket and his ladder swinging with his arm. Usually he was alone, but there were days and sometimes weeks at a time when a couple of village boys would walk with him and carry his ladder.

They had a purpose in going along, but aside from that it was pleasant to walk through the streets at this hour, with the dusk slowly closing in and diminishing the range of vision, while here and there a lamp came on in the houses. There was no hurry in the lamplighter's stride. In all his years of lighting the village he had taken in something of the serenity of dusk and nightfall. To stay beside him the boys had to curb their usual pace.

Sometimes even at this early hour they heard doors being barred and bolted for the night. For although no thief had been known to touch foot in the place within the memories of its oldest residents, everyone secured his house with such thoroughness, at the windows as well as the doors, that it would have taken a woodcutter with his axe to get at the treasures behind those Colijnsplaat facades. The boys walking through the streets took the sound for granted, as did the lamplighter, who would soon go home and do the same.

Their tour took them from the city hall down in Voorstraat—where they stopped midway to light the lamp in front of the burgomaster's house—then along the Doorpstraat and around to the area behind the church, known as Acter de Kerk. Here many of the farm laborers had their homes, as well as shopkeepers, with their small shops facing the street and living rooms at the rear. To the south, along the outskirts of the village, were garden plots owned or rented by the villagers. Here and there small stands of woodland provided sanctuary for nightingales and other birds; and because of the notes that soared from the trees these woodlands were called *Vogelgezang,* Bird Song. With the diminishing song in their ears the three with the ladder and matches turned north to light the rest of the town. The skipper's children, watching the lamp come on near their home, listening while their oldest sister sang for them a little song:

Nu branden zij de lantaarn,
De vonken vliegen er uit....

(Now they are lighting the lantern,
The flames are flying out....)

The matches the lamplighter used were an imported kind, much more efficient, the boys observed, than those used at home. Sometimes the old gentleman allowed them to strike one; they liked the way it burst immediately into flame. The matches they were accustomed to glowed quietly for some time, until finally the stick caught fire. And they had to be nursed along, cupped in one's hand, before they would do even that!

Whenever a matchbox was emptied it would be given to one of the boys as payment for service. They had a gentlemen's agreement among them to rotate turns so that each could earn a box. For boxes were not easily come by, and there was no end to the number of ways they could be used.

The night Jan earned his first matchbox was a red-letter day in his young life. He could not get home quickly enough, so eager he was to show his box to his brothers. The small wooden sliding drawer pleased him; he pushed it in and out. But what interested him even more was the diminutive colored picture on the label. There was a lighthouse, and there was a ship at sea.

Up in their room he and Adriaan and Marinus crowded around the flickering lamp on the table. Three dark heads bent over the little box and three pairs of dark eyes studied the scene. Then Adriaan, the oldest, read the impressive words: "Made in Sweden."

Beetles on Leash

In late spring or early summer, when the leaves were in full green and island earth teemed with life, the beetle fad swept through the village and caught every child in its spell. Boys climbed trees to catch the shiny insects as they sat close against the bark, and sold them for a penny to the girls and the very small children. No child had rest until he owned a pair. They tucked them into a small box or a baking powder can or whatever container they could get hold of, with holes punched in for air, a tuft of grass for a bed, and a sprig of small white wild blossom for food. Of course the boys who had matchboxes used those.

Wherever the children went they carried their pets. During their hours of play they would gather in the street and, tying a long, generous thread to a hind leg, set their beetles on the ground and walk with them. If they spread their wings and flew, the owners ran to keep up with them, giving out line as though they were flying kites. The yards and yards of thread that had come off a mother's sewing spool gave a beetle plenty of play, and they would fly far into the air. Jan had many go up and never come down; for the swallows often darted out of the linden trees and snatched the beetles in flight.

Competition and rivalry ran high among the beetle fans, especially among the boys, and this led to a great deal of discussion and argument and boasting as to who had the best beetles—the largest or the swiftest or the most perfectly formed. And with their imaginations working overtime they became so convinced by their own inflated talk that when they traded they were as solemn and deliberate as Amsterdam diamond dealers.

As suddenly as it had come the fever died out. Boys who had climbed trees to capture their beetles now climbed back to set them in some cozy crotch, satisfied that they were restoring to them all their rights and privileges. The grassy beds and the rations of flowers so carefully placed in the small cages were unceremoniously tossed. And the spools in the mothers' sewing baskets lay once more undisturbed.

Sunday

Until church time on Sunday mornings Colijnsplaat was as quiet as an abandoned town; not a footfall sounded in the streets, not a sail was hoisted in the harbor. But within the houses, behind those glittering windows and those scrubbed doorsteps, the air hummed with preparations for the approaching services.

While the men and boys waited in their dark suits, their feet in the leather shoes that had been polished for them the day before, the women and girls put on with care the dresses that had hung untouched for the past six days, and the jewels that had rested as long in their cases. Elizabeth DeJonge, in her best black silk, tied on a black taffeta apron and fastened at her throat her choker of garnets. The stones appeared almost black until a strong light shone through them, when they warmed to a rich transparent red. Into her *sak* under the slit in her dress she dropped her silver *snuf doosje*, its tiny enclosed sponge moist with cologne, and her silver *pepermunt doosje* filled with mint-flavored tablets.

Over in the house that faced the dike Adriana, the skipper's oldest daughter, sat before a mirror between two windows in the living room and put on her crisp white cap. Then she opened a small red box containing her gold ornaments. Her small sister Maria watched as, piece by piece, she hooked them on at her temples—the flat *spellen,* the spiral *krullen,* and the pendant hollow *bellen.* Now she was dressed.

A visitor out strolling on a Sunday morning might have observed among the folk walking to church an old lady with two young girls. The lady would have appeared replete with the dignity and weariness of age; but the energy of her youth accompanied her still in the persons of two small granddaughters.

Neeltje and Leun, who had become so attached to her when she made her home with them, liked to stop for their grandmother Breas and go with her to church. In their round straw hats and Kate Greenaway dresses, their lace-stitched stockings and shining black shoes, they walked demurely and happily beside her. *Mevrouw* Breas would be dressed in unrelieved black from her neck down, while on her head rested delicately her white cap. She was a true grootmoeder, mingling a kindly, gentle affection with her concern for the children. She carried her gold-clasped Bible; but the psalms she would sing from memory, for in the countless repetitions of a lifetime she had come to know them by heart.

Many families made their way to the State Church at the head of the Voorstraat, the oldest historic church of the Reformation. Its cornerstone proclaimed that the first stone had been laid by Prince Maurice, son of Prince William of Orange, sometimes called William the Silent.

The exterior walls were of colorless brick, worn by the seasons of centuries and clothed in an almost intangible garment of the sunshine and mist, rain, snow, and frost of all the vanished years.

At about a quarter to nine the De Jonge family would turn into the Dorpstraat and walk west—past the State Church and the Voorstraat and on to where the Achterweg took them north to the Separatist Church. Jan De Jonge's brown hair curled softly along his collar's edge, and across Elizabeth's shoulders fell the lace border of her cap. Their little girls wore at their throats their starched white dickies, or *beukjes,* and three-strand coral chokers. In the white pockets under their dresses they carried their pennies for the offering and their starched handkerchiefs, fine and crisp as paper and folded in precise squares.

Into the white interior of the church the soft morning light sifted through unstained glass. The De Jonges took their places in their rented pews—Elizabeth and her children in the center section and her husband in one of the outer pews, where the men sat with their older sons. Soon the skipper's family would come in and go their separate ways. Jan, sitting in the center with his mother or grandmother, his sisters and brother Marinus, would look longingly over to where Adriaan sat with their father, and contemplate the few years that would have to pass before he was eight and could sit like a man among the men.

Gradually the pews filled. Meanwhile Jan entertained himself identifying the people as they came in, sorting the men out in his mind as farmers and townsmen, landsmen and seamen. The costumes of the prosperous farmers fascinated him—their broad-brimmed beaver hats, their short black waistcoats, and most of all the big silver medallions that studded their wide leather belts.

On entering his pew a man would stand for a moment of devotions, his head bowed and his hat covering his face. Jan noticed how the skippers, who wore black dress caps to church, would hold them up by the visor, while the other men held their hats by the crown. One old gentleman whose white hair stood out bush-like from the sides of his head made an interesting picture as he held his hat before his face; and because he always remained in this attitude longer than the others Jan concluded that he must be superior in piety.

A little before nine o'clock the door to the right of the pulpit opened, and the minister, the song leader, and the elders and deacons filed in. The latter went to their prominent seats at right angles to the outer pews, while Dominie Schoolland ascended the narrow, curved stairway to his pulpit. Along the edge of the sounding board over him a verse from the Revelation stood out in gold: "He that hath an ear, let him hear what the Spirit saith unto the churches."

In the almost palpable silence of the filled sanctuary Kees Douw, standing at his lectern, unhooked the clasps of the big Bible and found the page for the Scripture reading to precede the sermon. Then, opening his psalter, he announced the first song, waited while the leaves of all the psalmbooks fluttered to the page, and with his strong, confident voice led the congregation in a swelling flow of worship and praise. The psalms were sung to long, whole notes that invested the singing with great solemnity and power.

During a later song, when the offering was to be taken, the deacons came up the aisles with black velvet bags on long poles. They would ease a bag into a pew, allowing just enough time for each person to drop in his coin, then lift it in a high arc over the row of heads and draw it back down the next pew. From the tip of the bag swung a black silk tassel.

For the little girls in their stiff dickies and closefitting corals with wide gold clasps, the hours in church in midsummer could be trying. But no thought of comfort ever tempted them to leave their corals at home. Jo would wipe her moist face with her folded handkerchief and received gratefully from her mother a few pepermuntjes. For Elizabeth there was always a sniff of cologne before settling down to listen to the long sermon, and sometimes she passed the snuf docsje to her children.

Here and there in the congregation men who caught themselves nodding would rise to their feet and force themselves to listen. Often by the time the service ended several men were standing. But this was taken for granted by all except the children, who wondered how anyone could possibly sleep so early in the day.

After the noon dinner, many of the adults and older children went back for the *middag* service. Those who stayed home closed the blinds on the windows facing the street and provided the children with some quiet pastime. Jan De Jonge spent the afternoon reading to his young ones; but what he read often went over their heads, and they would turn to their own amusements, improvising little games and activities while he went on and on, completely absorbed in his reading.

The skipper's boys, Adriaan, Marinus, and Jan, went for long walks on the dike and returned just in time for the Sunday night supper, the most *gezellig* or cozy and intimate of all their meals, with their father handsome in his navy blues and Moeder and their sisters glowing in the prettiness of their best clothes and their jewelry. On the table there would be the traditional Sunday night treats—white bread, spiced cheese, called *komijnekaas,* currant bread, and honey cake. With the tea there would be sugar to sweeten the first cup and anise squares for the second.

Once more in the evening the faithful gathered in their pews and psalms floated on the village air. Those who stayed at home with sleepy children closed their blinds and guarded their thoughts.

And when the last chorale of the day was sung and the benediction pronounced, the carriage wheels of the wealthy farmers rolled out of town and the footfalls of those who walked sounded for a while in the streets. Then all was quiet once more.

Churchgoers leaving the "kerk"; origin unknown.

Under the Lindens

When the city fathers planted the lindens along the Voorstraat they little dreamed that in the years to come the carefully spaced trees would have a part in keeping the citizens warm in winter as well as cool in summer. A summer shade they would eventually be, and a source of beauty and grace, softening the hard architectural lines of shops and houses, and arching the walks with a canopy of living green. But their relatedness to warmth was an accidental link brought about through a caprice of the young girls of the village.

It was under the linden trees that they gathered in small cliques to do the endless knitting their mothers pushed upon them. And the socks and mittens and even undershirts that came into being under those trees, could they be assembled, would make a towering tribute to the girls of Colijnsplaat.

Jannetje and Jo with their crowd, and Leun and Maria, who were a little older, with theirs—did just as other generations had done before them. Starting at one end of the Voorstraat, they stopped under each linden to knit a row. Down one side of the street and up the other they moved, their needles and their tongues flying.

Elizabeth De Jonge gave her daughters bits of colored yarn to insert in their work as markers. *Bratjes,* they were called. The girls were enchanted with their rich, bright colors and soft textures. With the bratjes in their knitting they could look back and see how far they had come within a given time. Sometimes they held races, each putting in a marker and then knitting furiously until the timekeeper called "Stop!"

Leun and Maria in fresh pinafores knitted on the Voorstraat every Saturday morning, whether the wind blew cold from over the sea or the sun baked the tile roofs of the town. By the time they finished the last tree on the second side of the street the lunch hour had arrived, and they could run home and tuck the needles and wool away—out of sight and out of mind.

In the Colijnsplaat school the teacher who gave sewing lessons taught knitting, too. But the village also provided another place where girls could go to learn new stitches and patterns. The *stovè* was a low, partially underground building where *madder* was raised for dyes. The owner and his family had living rooms in the odd-looking structure, and here his wife held lessons in knitting. Jannetje and Jo were among those who went one afternoon each week after school. The woman would go from one child to another, patiently giving instruction. Usually there was no break in the session of toil, but one day she offered her class some unusual refreshment; she passed a plate of freshly-boiled liver cut in small pieces. Their pig had been butchered that morning.

When Jo first began to knit she watched her mother and wondered whether she would ever be able to move her needles with such marvelous speed. Elizabeth's steel needles twinkled and clicked, flashing in and out of the wool like lightning among clouds. And always her right needle was tucked firmly under her arm. All the village women knitted that way. It gave the hand freedom for throwing the yarn over the needle. And when their needles were too short to reach from hand to armpit they used a wooden extension that looked like a small carved spindle; it had a hole drilled into one end for inserting the needle.

And so Jo tucked her needle under her arm. Up and down the Voorstraat she moved, putting in her bratjes and counting her rows, and after some seasons the day came when her needles flashed and clicked like her mother's, and her hands grew dexterous at whirring up a mitten and shaping the curves of an arch and a heel.

The Kermis

Every summer, in July, when the village drowsed in the sun's warmth, the kermis came and dispelled for a week or two its dreamy, comfortable languor.

The children were transported with delight; the feet that turned most naturally toward the harbor and the dike for hours of play now turned inland, clattering up the Voorstraat to where the carousel stood like a gaudy jewel under the linden trees.

On the opening day the children hurried to the outskirts of the village to break branches from the knotty willows that grew beside the streams and ditches. With these in their hands they gathered at the head of the Voorstraat and formed ranks for their annual parade through the village streets. Waving their green fronds aloft, they sang as they went—"Wien't Ne'erlands Bloed," "Wilhelmus van Nassauwe," "Piet Hein," and other national hymns and folk songs. Many people deplored the coming of the kermis and would have no part of it; but housewives hearing the singing in the streets went to the door to look out, and found pleasure in this innocent prelude to the vain affair.

The very heart and center of the kermis—for the children, at least—was the carousel. All color and movement and sound, it seemed a living, breathing thing. Even when

The carousel at the kermis; origin unknown.

it stood still the lions and zebras looked alive, awaiting only the master's word to break into a prance. Its scalloped top was splendid with beadwork and embroidery, and the area where the passengers rode glittered with mirrors and ornate lanterns that reflected and exaggerated the colors and designs in the brightly-worked velvet banners. You could ride a ferocious lion for four cents, or a horse or zebra for three cents, or if you were very young or very old you could sit serenely in a boat with three other passengers and go around for two pennies.

Since Jan and Elizabeth De Jonge were among those who disapproved of the kermis, little Jo had nothing to spend at the booths and tents on the Voorstraat, and no access to the wonderful carousel. But one day her Uncle Gerard, bringing her and her sisters home from a day in the country, set Jannetje and Jo, Prien and Margrieta, each on the mount of their choice, and away they went, passengers at last, the music being played for them, the great round floor spinning faster and faster—for them.

The lack of pennies in her pocket did not dampen Jo's enthusiasm for the kermis. Moeder had not forbidden her to go near the place, and she and her sisters mingled freely with the crowds who strolled on the Voorstraat. One booth in particular drew her again and again. Here sat rows of pert, wide-eyed dolls, waiting for someone to buy them. Their faces and clothes absorbed her attention, and she noticed how the caps and costumes varied as they represented the different provinces. She wondered what it would be like to own so perfect a doll; but the possibility was too remote to be disturbing.

So she walked among the sights and sounds and smells, the very unattainableness of everything preserving for her the wonder and strangeness of it all.

In one of the booths that lined the middle of the street the gypsies sold little soft, flat cakes like pancakes—*broedertjes,* they were called. Jan Merizon's sister Leun and her cousin Joppa spent every penny they could get on broedertjes. For their carousel rides they waited until evening, when they'd hop on just as the big disc began to turn, and crouch behind a boat. If the owner discovered them he shooed them off with a scolding.

Their sister Neeltje wouldn't have dreamed of doing such a thing. Her favorite haunt was the waffle booth, where you could buy crisp, golden squares so thin you could almost see through them. Hot from the iron, they were spread with butter and sprinkled with sugar, and you ate them like a cookie.

The largest of all the tents of the kermis stood on the Dorpstraat directly in front of the parsonage. Here the vaudeville acts were put on. There were trapeze stunts and tumbling acts and clever calisthenics. One solo act in particular made the young boys sit up and stare. A man in an embroidered white top and purple shorts would leap up on a huge white ball and roll it with his feet. Round and round in a wide circle he went—faster and faster, leaning at a perilous angle from the speeding ball. Jan had only one word for him. He was *kolossal.*

And then there was a magician who pulled a rabbit out of an empty hat. Brothers Adriaan and Jan were completely mystified. The only plausible conclusion they could come to was that the man must be in league with the devil.

When the pennies begged from fathers and mothers, grandmothers, grandfathers, and uncles were gone the boys of the village invariably went back to the carousel, offering their help and so earning a ride. At the center of the round platform a wide circular hole was hidden from view by a curtain. Here the boys disappeared for work. They stood on the brick pavement, and when the signal came they each took hold of an upright and began to push. Slowly the platform gained momentum, until finally the boys would be trotting at a brisk pace, while the mechanical organ sent out its blithe, weird tunes. When the carousel seemed to be whirling under its own speed the boys hopped on for their ride. But all too soon the big disc began to slow down. A little more coasting, a little more of letting the old cat die, and they would see the boss's head between the parted curtains signaling his crew to put on the brake. A slab of wood on an iron chain was dropped to the road, and two of the boys would jump on it. The notes of the organ died away as the scraping sound of the brake announced to the passengers the end of the tuneful ride.

At noon and during the supper hour the tents of the gypsies gave out the heavy aromas of their highly-seasoned foods. Children walking by on their way home would take deep, hungry breaths and try to analyze the smells.

To Jan these secretive, olive-skinned people were of a world apart. He would look at the long, thick hair falling over the shoulders of the children and wonder, Who were these people?...and, in what distant land would they make their home after they had finished their long, long travels?

When the day of departure for the kermis arrived and the carousel was taken down, the children watched its dismantling wistfully. Piece by piece the canopy was lifted and folded and packed into heavy wooden chests. Then the lions, the tigers, the horses...with the breaking down of the carousel the whole spirit of kermis seemed to collapse.

In a surprisingly short time the Voorstraat stood empty and still, and as the children watched the last boatload sail away a feeling of flatness lay on their spirits. Mischievous Leun felt that now surely all the fun of their lives had departed. What on earth would there be to do until the kermis came back another year!

Burned Letters

The kermis that came in Adriana's nineteenth year left a weight on her heart that would not be lifted. Even her young sisters Neeltje and Leun could feel that something was wrong.

One of the boats that sailed into Colijnsplaat was a river freighter owned by the widow Van Gelderen, who with her two sons carried on the business her husband had left her when he died.

Whenever the Van Gelderen barge, which was also the family home, dropped anchor at Colijnsplaat there was a flutter in the house that faced the dike. "Jana," as she was familiarly known, combed her dark hair and adjusted her cap, meanwhile keeping an eye out the window for the approach of a blond young skipper.

The widow was related to the Merizons, and the children of the two families had known each other from early childhood. But the Van Gelderen girls took little interest in their village cousins; they regarded them and all of Colijnsplaat as hopelessly provincial. One had to get around. To their surprise and annoyance their brother Adriaan lost his heart to Jana, and soon the engagement was announced.

The kermis was coming to Colijnsplaat, and Jana was looking forward to having Adriaan with her for most of the week. Then, at the last moment, word came that he would not be able to come. Jana plunged into a state of gloom. What would the kermis be without him. And why couldn't Adriaan arrange his business just this once to accommodate something so important. She would not go to the kermis.

But the village grapevine hummed, and one of the boys who heard of Jana's plight decided to take a hand. He had a way with him, and besides, who could resist the kermis! Almost before she knew what was happening Jana was caught up in the holiday mood.

It was a week of fun, but when the excitement was over and the days settled back to their normal routine the girl began to wonder. Had she been wise? Would Adriaan think she had been fickle and untrue? If she didn't write him he was certain to hear about it anyway, for there was that girl with a loose tongue whose father also sailed a boat and often met the Van Gelderens. Jana tormented herself with questions and fell into a state of anxiety and regret. Sometimes her mother came upon her crying.

"You must write and tell him," Lavina said firmly. "Come." And she laid paper and pen before the brooding girl. Jana gazed out through the window and bit the pen holder as she composed her lines, her arched brows, so like her mother's, lifted above thoughtful eyes. She said what she had to say, and when finally she sealed and posted

Adriana Merizon

the letter the world seemed a more hopeful place. Adriaan's reply was reassuring, and all seemed well.

For a time life went on serenely. Jana, easy with herself now, and confident, looked forward to his next visit. But one day the envious friend had a piece of news for her. Adriaan, she confided, had been seen in one of his distant ports with a girl!

With a girl. It was tit for tat then. Adriaan did care that she had gone to the kermis with someone else. Jana left her tormentor and hurried blindly home. And to think he had written her that everything would be all right. Oh! But it was her fault, she told herself mercilessly. Now all the feelings of anxiety and regret returned and engulfed her once more, this time in a sea of despair. And along with the despair there was anger—against Adriaan and the gossips and her own vulnerable self.

In her room she took from a drawer the small pack of letters she had treasured and kept carefully in this one place. Without considering, or entertaining any possibility of a change of mood or a new understanding, she went quickly to the kitchen and dropped the letters into the stove.

Adriaan came again, and later, again. But something had gone out of Jana in her relationship with him. His visits grew farther and farther apart, until the time came when she knew they were saying goodbye for the last time.

The Bleach

On wash days the green lawns behind the houses were almost hidden beneath a white mosaic. The linens and other pieces lay flat on the earth, exposed to the sun for hours—not only to dry but to grow still whiter, if that were possible. So important was this weekly sunning that the lawn was called *de blijk*—the bleach.

Elizabeth De Jonge, living on the Achterstraat, had a deep lawn stretching away from her kitchen door. She could spread her wash unhampered. But behind the house that faced the dike the yard was like a handkerchief, and Lavina spread only her smaller things on the grass. She had a little box of clean, smooth stones that the children had gathered for her; these she laid on the pieces to anchor them in place. The rest of her wash she hung over long poles that fit into slots in posts. On windy days she had to pin the lapped-over sides of the sheets together to keep them from flying away.

Often when her wash was too large for the little bleaching yard and the poles, she would carry a basketful to the dike with one of her girls and spread things out on the seaward side—if the wind was not too wild. The grassy slope, catching the high summer sun or its suffused light in the immense sky, was a perfect place for a wash to bake slowly dry. Under the sun's wide arc its whiteness was renewed; and when it was gathered up and carried in, the clean cotton and linen smells were shot through with aromas of salt sea air and sun warmth.

A Shoe Could Be a Ship

On the street behind the State Church, and facing the moat that surrounded the centuries-old churchyard, stood the little shop where the klompen-maker carved new shoes out of poplar wood and mended his customers' worn ones. There were always some small-sized klompen waiting to be repaired, for the children especially were hard on their stiff, unyielding footwear. Many a shoe went out of the shop wearing a strip or two of tin to hold it together.

But there came a time in the life of every wooden shoe when nothing more could be done for it. Most klompen undoubtedly met some obscure, inconsequential end, but the worn-out shoes in the skippers' families went on to grander destinies. The boys made sailing ships of them and launched them in battle.

When Jan came into possession of a cast-off shoe he would hurry over to his grandfather's shop. "Bobba" lived around the corner to the east, on the Achterstraat; his shop stood back from the house, beyond the green stretch of lawn.

He was a tall, slim man, and he walked with a limp acquired in a fall from a mast in the days of his prime as a shipwright. In retiring from his work on the waterfront he had unconsciously brought into his small workshop as much of the sea as was possible. He made water casks for boats, and masts cut of the pliant riga wood. From broken masts brought in by skippers he made smaller ones, cutting them down and tapering them, and planing them smooth by hand. On the walls of the shop and strewn over the workbench were the tools of his craft—planes, saws, adzes, hammers, and other shapes that had become so familiar to Jan's eyes.

As the boy entered the shop the clean, sharp odor of raw wood greeted him. There was no need to explain why he had come, when he carried a shoe in his hand. That his grandson should want to make a sailing ship was to Marinus the most natural thing in the world—as much to be expected as that he should walk, or breathe. Dropping whatever he was doing, the grandfather would take his drawknife and cut off the top of the shoe, sloping it up toward the front. Next he built a little deck fore and aft, and in the forward deck he carved out a notch where the mast should stand. When the notch was carved the boat was handed back to Jan, and so he went home to work on the mainsail, the boom, and the jib. These had to be done in the authentic way, for Skipper Adriaan never allowed his sons to make one of the little boats haphazardly. If they tried to get by with careless work or shortcuts he would take the boat in his hand and look at it dubiously, then at the boy questioningly, as if to say, "And what do you call that?"

They could not with any sense of integrity simply

fasten the sails or halyards down permanently to the hull. They had to provide the wooden blocks for the halyards to pass through. To this end Jan hoarded the pits of all the cherries he ate during the cherry season. Then whenever he was ready to put up the rigging on a new boat he would thrust a handful of the pits into his pocket and go over to Bobba's shop. There on the big grindstone, which he had to turn by hand, he ground holes through opposite sides of the hard outer shells. After a pit was ground on two sides he picked out the soft inner kernel and laid the shell carefully aside. A boat required about sixteen to eighteen of these, and it was no small task to turn that enormous wheel with one hand and hold the tiny cherry pit hard against the revolving stone with the other. The tips of his lefthand fingers were raw when he finished.

In spite of the hours of painstaking work, a boat never sat around long as an ornament or piece of handcraft. As soon as several boys had boats completed they would go down to the water's edge at high tide, fill their pockets with pebbles, and, if the sea was calm, set the boats adrift. Usually, however, the sea was too rough, and after gathering pebbles they went to a pond just east of the village, close to the dike. There the little ships glided before the wind, and the boys would run along the shore pelting enemy ships while keeping an anxious eye on their own. No matter the care, the love, the toil that had gone into their making—they were bombarded, maimed, annihilated, until one alone survived, sails still aloft. This was the crowning moment for her captain, worth the sore fingers and the exacting toil. But the battle itself, after all, had been the best part.

The King's Path

Past the pond where the boys sailed their boats a granite walk came down from the dike to meet the road. A stranger looking seaward from the crest of the wall might have wondered why the walk should be there. The shore below was without dock or inlet or other accommodation for traffic.

But sometime around 1870 a ship bearing the royal ensign had anchored here. William the Third, on a tour of the lowlands, had stopped off at North Beveland, disembarking at Colijnsplaat.

His coming was anticipated weeks in advance, and the village officials laid careful plans for the event. They decided that the royal visitor should not enter their town along the way frequented by ordinary commerce; in his honor and for his convenience they laid this special granite walk, about a quarter of a mile east of the harbor.

Here the splendid procession had passed, and here the islanders had gathered to welcome their exalted visitor. But after William's departure the walk fell into disuse; and although it became a landmark and was proudly referred to as *de Koning's Padje*—the King's Path, sea-loving plants and weeds gradually effaced from view the end that dipped down to the sea. The children who played on the dike knew exactly where it was and instinctively avoided it, for under the tangle of green that lay innocently upon it a coating of moisture and microscopic vegetation made the granite as slippery as ice under snow.

One day when Jan and Adriaan with their friends were chasing over the dike and throwing jellyfish like custards at one another, Jan in his excitement forgot where he was. He ran onto the King's Path and slid promptly into the sea. The tide was going out and the receding water carried him away from the dike.

Marinus stood sobbing and helpless. But Len Koole with a quick eye discovered a long stick lying nearby, and taking it down as far as he could thrust it out to Jan, calling to him to take hold. The help came just in time.

Back on shore, Jan was surrounded by a frightened circle regarding him with a kind of awe. As he lingered there in the sun to dry himself off he looked at his feet ruefully and wriggled his toes. He would have to go home and break the news to his mother: His klompen had gone out with the tide.

The Bell Tolls

There were five girls and one boy in the family of Jan and Elizabeth De Jonge when Neeltje the baby died. Suddenly the house, so constantly a place of chatter and movement, was smitten with silence. Jannetje and Jo, Margrieta and Prien, spoke in subdued voices and moved about quietly.

The little girls had often watched the *lijkbidder* go solemnly from house to house with a message of death, and had seen him stand at their own door to make a mournful announcement. Now he would be going on his rounds for their family. He would call at the homes of their friends and relations and announce in a singsong voice that Neeltje, the year-old daughter of Jan and Elizabeth De Jonge, had died. He would give the day and hour of the funeral and then leave to repeat the same words at the next place. In his long black cape and high-crowned hat he was a grim figure; wherever he went the children stared at him. Mr. Buys was the lijkbidder for the members of the

Separatist Church. The State Reformed Church engaged Adriaan De Waard.

A funeral announcer, the lijkbidder. Origin unknown.

The children were expected not to go out and forget themselves in play during these few days, and the hours dragged by in a strange, bleak void. Their mother cared for them as usual but spoke so little and appeared so preoccupied that they felt not only that they had lost their baby sister, but that Moeder had somehow withdrawn from them the part of herself they most needed. And when they came upon her kneeling beside the tiny casket in the alcove, weeping, their desolation was unbounded.

The hour for the service finally drew near. The four sisters stood about shyly in the hall and front rooms, where they could watch the guests arrive. Nom "Sias" and Moe Prien came, of course, from the mill, and with them some of their older sons and daughters. There was Nom Gerard, who had a beautiful farm west of the village, with gooseberries striped and plump and sharp to the taste, and currants like scarlet glass balls. It was Nom Gerard who had given them a ride on the carousel. Nom Jacob and Moe Koba were there, from *achter de Kerk*; and even Nom Jan came, from Kortgene on the other side of the island; and Moe Neeltje from Wissenkerke, where Jannetje and Jo had once visited for a week. After a first day of homesickness they had filled the hours with play; but the one thing Jo remembered most vividly of their week at Wissenkerke was a violet dress that hung like something precious but mysteriously remote in the dim front parlor.

Moe Viena and Nom Marine with his wife, Mietje, had only to walk over from the Voorstraat. From overheard remarks the children had gathered that Moe Mietje had a great idea of herself and her ménage. It was even said that she nipped in the bud every romance her daughter had—that so far the young men who had walked the young Mietje home from church on Sunday evenings or from catechism had not come up to her mother's requirements. This was a puzzle to Jannetje and Jo; anyone who would interfere with so many romances must, they decided, be more than a little odd. But here was Moe Mietje in her black silk and her white cap, appearing in every way a person who knew exactly what she was about.

Nom Willem and Moe Wilhelmina came—from the farm where the host of daffodils bloomed in springtime, and where the great rocking horse stood in the center hall. And finally Dominie Schoolland, tall and slender and grey haired, with dignity in his bearing and compassion in his voice as he greeted the waiting family.

They gathered in a large room at the rear of the house, where the windows looked out on the bleaching green and the big barn beyond.

When the brief service was ended, amid the gentle pushing of chairs and the rustle of long skirts, the men left on foot for the burial ground out the New Mill Way. Jan wore the high silk hat he had so often loaned to friends and neighbors for similar processions. As they left the house and started down the street the bell in the school tower began to toll. Its sound accompanied them a good part of the way. Out over the still, level fields and the tossing sea the bell notes floated—notes that could on occasion sound joyous and alive but were now all expressive of pathos and resignation, and a somber, majestic hope.

In Elizabeth's kitchen her niece Tannetje and the maid hurried about preparing a lunch, setting out plates and cups and silver and filling trays with cakes and pastries. Soon the aroma of coffee drifted through the air, and Jannetje and Jo, following their adored cousin around, began to feel some of the heaviness go out of the house and a little of its pleasantness return. And when their father came in and laid aside his high silk hat it seemed that the terrifying episode was closed. Life could begin to go on once more in its usual way.

Surely, they thought, with all these kind people around her Moeder must feel consoled. Elizabeth held little Johannes, not yet three, on her lap as she talked with her sisters.

It was not too disturbing to the children when at first here and there an aunt or a cousin rose and murmured, "Wij moeten vertrekken...," for there was still a wealth of company about them seemingly in no particular hurry to go. But when as the afternoon wore on the ranks began to thin and it was evident that soon the family would be left alone with their sorrow, the feeling of desolation descended again, and they watched wistfully each departing carriage. If only Tannetje would stay!

It was like Tannetje to let her family go home without her, to stay and prepare supper and in her own way to pick up the links of the broken chain and hold them together in a new, smaller circlet—to tuck the children into their alcove beds, telling them a story and singing a pretty song, and then sitting with Nom Jan and Moe Betje for a while until the carriage from the house beside the mill should come for her. Elizabeth always said that Tannetje was more like a sister than a niece.

Sometime in the days that followed, and before she again stepped out of her house in formal dress, Elizabeth removed from her white cap the border of Brussels lace and replaced it with a plain white band.

Hunters from France

Every year in the fall, when the fields were shorn of their crops and farmers had closed their stock in for the winter, a party of hunters from France came to the island to shoot Belgian hares.

From the hotel the advance news of their coming spread abroad through town and countryside, and on the night of their arrival many islanders stayed up past their usual hour to gather at the harbor and watch the party come in.

The hunters came from as far as Schouwen on a chartered steamer, then tranferred at the port of Zierikzee to Karremann's ferry. Around ten o'clock the waiting throng would spy a cluster of lights heading toward the harbor, and suddenly as the ferry drew nearer a burst of fireworks rose from her deck. Skyrockets soared into the night sky and broke in showers of stars, and pinwheels made golden circles in the darkness. The children were entranced—but not they alone; some of the fathers and mothers had looked forward all day to this rare hour of enchantment.

Mijnheer Eekman from the Achterstraat would be among the small group who officially greeted the sportsmen, for he spoke French and would be their guide and interpreter during their stay. In their fashionable hunting costumes the men drew all eyes toward them as they made their way among the knots of people to the Hotel de Patrijs. Behind them followed their porters, carrying guns and baggage.

Soon after the door had closed on the last pair of foreign boots the harbor area lay deserted and still. The only movement was the slap of water against the quay and the hulls of anchored boats.

Hotel de Patrijs, Colijnsplaat; origin unknown.

For the next few moments the little streets under the starlight were curiously alive with footbeats as families and solitary ones trooped home to bed.

To the thrifty and industrious islanders the privilege of shooting a few hares was hardly worth the cost of gun and hunting license; and so the men from France, who owned mortgages on some of the farms through banks in Rotterdam and Dort, found plenty of game in the fields and thickets of North Beveland. Often when they came in from a day of gunning the wheelbarrows their porters pushed were heaped with hares. Sometimes a lone huntsman would stride past the house that faced the dike, on his way to the hotel, with a hare or two swinging from a stick over his shoulder. The thoughtful Neeltje observed the long, limp bodies with pity, but at the same time noted with pleasure the tan corduroy coat, the blue velvet breeches, and the polished leather leggings of the hunter.

All day, wherever they went, the children kept their eyes open for empty cartridges—the little blue or red paper shells with brass caps. Usually the smell of gunpowder was still fresh upon them, and the sharp odor came to be associated in their minds with the handsome, pleasure-loving men who had brought them. Occasionally when a group of children followed the huntsmen to the edge of town, hoping for a few scattered paper shells, suddenly a shower of pennies would fly through the air and fall at their feet.

The hunters brought their own chef with them, and their own wines, and the few businessmen of the Voorstraat who were their guests at dinner for one gala evening had something to tell their customers when shops opened the next morning.

After a few days of the sport the men boarded the ferry and sailed for their steamer at Zierikzee, taking with them a good supply of dressed hares for their tables in France.

The children of Colijnsplaat laid their blue and red shells on a dresser or table, souvenirs to be kept unmolested and once in a while taken up and sniffed. What had happened every year in the past would, they were confident, take place again. There would be the fireworks, and the ingratiating men with their guns, and perhaps best of all, the strange and pleasant excitement that quickened the village when they were there.

Pork for the Winter

As the warmth of late summer gave way to chilling winds and cold nights the thought of the housewives turned to their winter supplies, and they began making engagements with the butcher for the annual pig killings. It was a holiday for the children of a family when their pig was to be butchered; they were allowed to stay home from school.

At about eight o'clock in the morning the procession would go through the streets—the butcher with a pack of straw on his back, leading the pig on a leash, his assistant pushing a two-wheeled cart, and a troop of children, all on their way to the clearing outside the town.

The pig was quickly killed and then plucked. The boys of the family who owned the animal tussled with one another to get at the best bristles on its back. They would trade them at the *schoenmaker's* for black Norwegian pitch, which they chewed like gum. The shoemaker used the pitch for waxing his thread and for blending two or three strands into one strong cord; but he was always ready for a trade. The bristles made excellent needles for sewing in leather, after the holes had been punched with an awl.

When the pig was plucked the straw was laid around him, and a quick fire singed the hide smooth. Then buckets of water from the nearby creek were poured over the blackened skin, and the hide was scraped with a metal scraper. Last of all it was scrubbed with a stiff brush until it shone white and glistening. In this state the pig was trundled back to the house. He was followed by the owner's children and any others who were too young for school or had managed to stay home that day.

In the kitchen or on the spacious floor of the barn the cutting-up began, and the processing of the meat went on for the rest of the day. A youthful audience would gather, wide-eyed and full of hushed comments, and then rush out to play. But their curiosity brought them back again and again. Such knives the butchers had! And saws, and cleavers, and a grinder to chop the sausage meat. One of the men spent a long time pushing the ground sausage into the long tubular skins.

By evening all the various cuts and products were spread out in a grand display—hams and steaks and sausages, head cheese, pork to be put in brine, and fresh side pork. Nothing was wasted. The heart and liver along with a cut of tastier meat were taken to one of the homes where there was no pig. And all looked forward to that first fresh pork dinner of the season.

Ice on the Moat

When winter came the stagnant, useless ribbon of water that enclosed the ancient churchyard became suddenly a lively thoroughfare. It was shaped like the rim of a rectangle, with a piece cut along the Dorpstraat where the parsonage, the school, and the State Church stood side by side.

The ice on the moat had a peculiar quality; when it was not frozen to too great a depth it was remarkably flexible and would give under heavy pressure without cracking.

Afternoons as soon as school was out the boys would run to the moat at its nearest point, just east of the parsonage. Joining hands three or four abreast, they ran with all their weight in their klompen, and the ice would rise in front of them in a graceful swell. Always the swell moved ahead of them, and at each step the low, depressed area under their feet held, elastic and strong. The children called it *buig-ijs*—bend-ice—and knew from experience that the most flexible stretch was there beside the parsonage and around the corner along the east section.

There were many small sleighs or "push chairs" in the wintry traffic on the moat—and on the Voorstraat, too, when snow had fallen. The De Jonge family's maid willingly took the children, two at a time, for rides in their *ijs bak,* as they called their sleigh. The "ice box" was like a narrow cutter with two single seats facing each other and solid wooden sides that extended down to the runners. It had a certain grace about it; the high back curved outward at the top and became a handle for the one who pushed. The Colijnsplaat people made much of their sleighs, painting them in bright colors and decorating them with floral designs on the panels and striping along the edges.

To the smooth, solid surface of the moat and to the snowy Voorstraat the children came also with their *prikslees*—little sleds that were propelled with two short poles fitted at the tips with metal points. Sitting on their prikslees with their feet thrust out in front of them, or alert and up on their knees, they darted around at a rakish speed. They had a deft way of steering about and slithering between other sleds and sleighs when the traffic was heavy.

Jan had a prikslee of solid oak that Bobba had made for him in his workshop. It required more push than the lighter ones, but once going it seemed to carry itself along. Often the boys left their poles behind and dragged their sleds up to the top of the dike, then rode down at an angle on the seaward side and coasted along the leveled-off path that lay halfway up from the base. The top half of the exposed side of the dike, grassy in summer, was smooth for coasting in winter.

On Saturday all the skates in Colijnsplaat were up on their blades. One of the ponds was east of the village, some distance past Jan's home—the place where the boys sailed their wooden-shoe boats in summertime. It was simply a wild pond edged with cattails and surrounded by open fields, but because it belonged to Mijnheer Biebou, the burgomaster, it was elegantly called the *vijver,* a name usually reserved for a landscaped pool. The other skating pond lay west of the village between a broken-down outer dike and the newer one. It was formed of stagnant seawater and was called "The Trultus."

The skaters stooped in the cold wind to strap on their skates. Many of the small boys spent all their leisure time on the ice. When their straps wore out they simply tied a piece of rope here and another there and glided off. If snow had fallen, one of the big fellows took the *bezem*—a bundle of twigs tied to a stick—and swept the ice clean.

There was one skater in particular who made a great impression on the small children; he could write his name on the ice! In performing this feat he would swirl around and veer over so far, they were sure he was going to fall. But he never did.

Toon Koole was the only person in the village to flash around on a pair of metal skates. His father had bought them in Antwerp, and they had come from America. But no one seemed to envy him. "Metal? All metal?" the other boys would say. "But they must be heavy—way too heavy!" And looking at them askance they circled round and glided away on their wooden blocks.

At either pond, if in spite of all their handknit woolens they became chilled, the skaters could stop and enjoy a cup of hot chocolate or anise milk. It was served in small colored cups and sold for a penny at a little table under a tent at the edge of the ice.

Foot-Happy

On Saturday mornings Lavina scoured her children's klompen with pumice, and in wintertime she set them in the oven to dry. When they came out, bleached and hot, the children although eager to be out playing lingered over their dressing to feel the delicious sense of warmth their clean shoes gave them. And later, out in the bitter air, they kept toast-warm for hours because their feet were encased in those snug wooden pockets.

When the chill air in the house told Elizabeth De Jonge that the morning was colder than usual she heated her children's shoes before they left for school. After their breakfast of hot porridge they gathered round the stove in the living room, and Moeder would take hot coals and rattle them around in their klompen until a little of the heat was absorbed. The sight of the glowing coals in their shoes had such a comforting effect that the children were led to feel foot-warm for the rest of the day.

As far as protection went, the church in wintertime

was hardly more than a shelter against the wind and snow. On Sunday the floor of the center section was dotted with foot stoves, draped round with the long, full skirts of the women whose feet rested on them; while in the outer sections the men and older boys sat through the service without assuaging heat of any kind. Since the floor was of slate tile and as cold as a floor could be, the men often passed up their leather dress shoes and wore their klompen to church, the soles lined with a piece of wool cloth or carpeting.

Jo welcomed her turn to carry her mother's foot warmer to church. Her enjoyment was half anticipation, for she was sure that sometime during the service the stove would be unobtrusively pushed toward her, and she would know for a while the pleasure of having it all to herself. It was warm, like a stove, and it was little and low, like a footstool, and so gave her two kinds of comfort. Sometimes she would lean forward to peer through the holes cut in its wooden top, and there down in the dimness she would see the red-hot chunks of peat glowing in their metal cup.

From the house that faced the dike Jan started out Sunday mornings with his mother's stove swinging from his hand; if they stopped on the Voorstraat for Grootmoeder Betje he carried two of them. Until he was eight years old he sat in the center section with the women folk, of course, but whenever one of the foot warmers was smuggled along the pew he pushed it by with all the tradition behind him. He was training himself for a seat over there to the side, where the men sat in such splendid indifference to the cold. The nearer the time came for his eighth birthday, the more longingly he looked toward the place where Adriaan and Marinus sat beside their father.

The care the mothers showed for their children's comfort followed the small ones right to bed those chilly winter evenings. In the wool blanket that lay next to them Moeder made a wide fold across the foot to form a pocket for their feet. The children took their *voetekot* for granted, instinctively feeling for it as they slid down under their covers. And with their feet in harbor for the night they furled their sails and slept.

Round Loaves and Crusts

Lying in the very heart of Zeeland, long known as the granary of the nation, the wheat fields of North Beveland were a picture of grace and plentitude; from the alluvial soil that lay beneath them the wheat drew sustenance so rich that the stalks soared high into the air and bore long, plume-like ears packed with swelling kernels.

Most of the grain harvested on the island was shipped to brokers in Dort, but a good supply went to the two mills in Colijnsplaat. The hand-kneaded bread that was made from the wheat was good, satisfying bread; with a cup of tea and a piece of side pork it made a breakfast that stood by a man through long hours of work.

Lavina bought her whole wheat flour with the bran still in and sifted it herself, a small quantity at a time. The hearty light brown loaves were her family's everyday fare—their nourishment for work and play throughout the week. On Sundays and holidays they enjoyed creamy white bread, and often a raisin or currant loaf.

The two bakers on the Voorstraat made the bread for most of the village families. Lavina sent her flour to the one just around the corner, three doors from the hotel. The other bakeshop was at the opposite end of the street— at the corner of the Dorpstraat.

In the De Jonge home Elizabeth kept a special big round pan for carrying the flour away and the bread home. She would measure the flour into the pan, cover it with a white cloth, and send it off with one of the children to the shop on the corner. Often it was Jo who was asked to take it, and while talking with the baker and inquiring when the bread would be ready she sometimes heard the clatter of dishes and other sounds from the apartment adjoining the shop, where *de bakker* lived with his family. Because she never had occasion to go into those rooms but repeatedly heard the intimate domestic hum of the household, those living quarters had for her an intriguing atmosphere— always shut away from her experience yet provocatively near.

It was said by some that the bakers shaved just enough flour off each order to accumulate enough for their own families' needs; but it was said with a shrug and a twinkle, and no one seemed to mind—and besides, it could not be proved.

For the children, taking the flour to the baker was a routine and unrewarding errand. But going after the bread had its points, especially in winter, when the warm loaves in the round pan were like a gentle stove in the circle of their arms and the wonderful fragrance from the slow-baked crust made the coming meal beckon like a feast.

Usually one or more of the round loaves would come out a little lopsided, with a ridge standing out where the dough had spilled over the side; whoever went for the bread hoped for at least one such ridge to break off and eat on the way home. There was a tacit understanding about this, and mothers appeared not to notice when a loaf had been discreetly tampered with.

Jan made many a trip to the bakery that stood between his Uncle David's home and Dr. Berkenfeld's. When he and Marien Koole called for the bread and found a couple of promising crusts on the loaves, they strolled farther up the street to see if the grocer had set out an empty molasses barrel. The sea winds and the northern air gave all the children perpetual appetites, and between-meal treats were one of the joys of living. If a newly-emptied barrel stood out on the walk Marien would tip it while Jan pulled the bung and held the crusts under the spout. They knew that with a little maneuvering and some patient waiting they could coax out the last of the dark, sweet syrup. The slow stream finally trickled down and fell in a crooked line along the strips of bread, and the boys waited with difficulty while they carefully completed operations and set the barrel back.

Meanwhile the fresh loaves waited under their napkin, and little did Lavina dream, when later the pan was brought into the kitchen, that her bread had sat on the street for an interval while her son refreshed himself with broken-off crusts sweetened with molasses.

Saint Marten's Day

On Saint Marten's Day the laborers from the surrounding farms came into Colijnsplaat to renew their contracts for another year or to make agreements with new employers.

At the tavern beside the city hall master and hired man sat down together, and over their glasses of gin or brandywine, with a witness present, they made their verbal contract, the master asking for another year of service, the laborer promising to serve another year. Later in the day the masters would withdraw for a social gathering of their own—usually in the hotel.

Strolling in from all directions, the men created a pleasant stir in the village. The laborers were dressed in their best suits and leather shoes; the prosperous landowners wore imposing beaver tricorns and around their waists wide black leather belts studded with huge silver buttons.

The boys of the village believed with innocent logic that the wealthier a man was, the bigger would be the medallions on his belt. They had a busy time of it on Saint Marten's Day sizing up all the silver and deciding who was the richest man there.

A farmer and his belt of silver medallions. Origin unknown.

An Island Farm

One farmer who did not go into town and the tavern on Saint Marten's Day was Adriaan De Pree, the husband of Lavina's sister Elizabeth, known to her kin as Betje. Although of gracious disposition, Adriaan was reserved in manner and preferred to renew contracts with his two hired men without joining the throng in the village.

His farm lay west of the village and was reached by driving a short distance out the New Mill Way and then turning south. In the level, skyey countryside the farms lay not too far apart for neighborliness; but the easy pace of travel gave a feeling of spaciousness and distance, and it seemed quite a drive before one came to the De Pree house on the left side of the road, almost hidden from view by a tall, thick hedge. Turning in at the opening, one passed almost unnoticing over a stubby wooden bridge that spanned a narrow creek along the roadside.

The weathered white brick house with its tile roof

was familiar to all of Lavina's children, but especially to Neeltje, who spent more time there than any of her sisters and brothers. The seclusion and freedom of the countryside, the far vistas over fields and orchards, and the blithe company of her cousin Elizabeth satisfied certain needs within her. She would come and stay for weeks at a time. As she rode up the drive and walked in at the door the pearly light of the lowlands would be pouring in through the many large windows; and the rooms, shining and serene, gathered her in as one who had come to a second home.

At Tante Betje's, Neeltje was expected to rise at six or six-thirty for her breakfast of tea and bread and sausage, and to go to bed at half past eight. There was only one possible flaw in her life on the farm—if she could bring herself to admit such a thing. Supper was served at four-thirty in the afternoon. Although Neeltje was always ready for a slice of Moe Betje's delicious bread when the table was laid, the supper hour was much too early, for by the time she climbed into bed at half past eight she was hungry again.

Across the way from the farm and running parallel with the road and the creek, a dike lifted its high, sloping hump. It was an inner dike, a boundary and protecting wall between polders. It is possible that at one time it held back the waters of the sea, in the years after the floods of 1530 and 1532 when the island was slowly being reclaimed. Now the dike's contours were softened by a thick tufting of grass and flowering plants and by trees whose network of roots held the heaped earth in place. To the casual eye of a stranger seeing only a small portion of it the dike could have appeared a natural rise in the ground.

Every year in spring the slope was white with cowslips, and for days the flowering wall was like an embroidered scarf dropped on the green land. Then the petals withered and fell and the design seemed to fade into the earth. But buttercup roots were as plentiful here as cowslips; and soon they lifted their buds and spread their petals, and suddenly one morning the hillside was a bank of gold.

To Neeltje and Elizabeth the dike was ever an invitation to climb; they liked to stand on its leveled summit and look out over the grain fields, to where other clusters of buildings marked the life centers of other farms. The red-roofed houses and reed-thatched black barns lay snug and secure against the flat earth, appearing from this distance like toy buildings on a soft rug; but the hearth smoke pluming from their chimneys and figures moving about in the yards betrayed their human occupancy.

On the lawn of the wide white house four linden trees stood in a row, their round bases thickly bedded in small seashells. Running in from a watch on the wall, the girls liked to stop and scoop up a handful of the shells and study their exquisite shapes. If their delighted eyes fell on a pink one in the white drift, they felt as one who had come upon a treasure.

Most of the daylight hours they spent in the fields and gardens and buildings behind the house, where the green turf gave the farmyard a pleasant, meadow-like air. Ducks paddled in a small pond and climbed soberly onto the grass. A goat cropped the lawn around the tree where she was tethered. Kittens played about and sat down suddenly to wash themselves, while their elders dozed in the sun.

From the farmyard a drive led back into the fields,

passing on its left a high hedge with a wooden gate set in midway. Behind the hedge lay Tante Betje's fruit garden, where row upon row of bushes bore berries of many colors and flavors. It seemed to the children in early summer a kind of enchanted place, with its leafy walls too high to see over and only the great soft sky above—and hanging on the bushes gooseberries as big as plums, red ones and green ones, plump and round and delicately striped, like blown-glass ornaments on some fairy tree.

The moist air and the rich, damp earth of Zeeland made berries grow to extravagant size, and the currants in the garden, like the berries, were swollen to great proportions. Among their green leaves the glossy clusters shone temptingly—scarlet on some bushes, and on others green, or black.

Beyond the garden were the orchards, where pear and apple trees dropped their fruit in the shaggy grass of late summer—small sugar pears, called *yutten,* and normal-sized pears; and apples—bright red *wijn* and strawberry apples, and delicious long green ones called *ribbelingen.* It was a place where children could feast as they ran. Sometimes the two girls heaped a basket high with the bright harvest and carried it between them to the house.

As they crossed the yard they would be greeted by Snip the dog. His kennel was a barrel tipped on its side and cemented in place, with a brick pavement at its opening to serve as courtyard, dining table, and general lookout. Snip was a sergeant at arms among the farmyard population.

Neeltje's gentle ways enabled her to make pets of all the animals. She learned to milk the goat, and carried the small, rich yield to the house in a gray granite pan. Later it would appear on the table as coffee cream. The cows she called by name—Bonti and Mol, Tip and Tiger. She and Elizabeth often helped Adriaan or one of the hired men with the milking, which was done out in the pasture as long as the weather was mild. Sometimes they took a notion to curry the four big placid creatures. They gave each

Zeeland girls milking cows. Origin unknown.

a complete going-over, first with a comb and then with a brush, while the beasts stood quiet and willing, seeming to enjoy the attention.

It was Neeltje and Elizabeth who taught the calves to drink from a pail. They would scoop up a little milk in their hands and lift it to the calves' lips. Gradually they coaxed them to bend lower and lower, until finally they were lapping the milk from the pail.

In the loft of the barn the two young things in pinafores had good, satisfying sessions of jumping and bouncing in the hay, keeping step oftentimes to the rhythm of a little song—

Francelina ging eens wandelen
En zij nam haar sussie mee...

(Francelina once went walking
And she took her sister with her...)

One day Elizabeth laid a ladder across the opening in the high floor and ran gaily over it, calling to her cousin to follow. But Neeltje's dress caught on something at the edge of the loft, and down she plunged, just missing one of the cows and hitting the floor with a fearful thud. Elizabeth, terrified, ran away and hid, while Neeltje in a daze slowly picked herself up.

The wagon house beside the barn was another intriguing place for climbing and jumping, and there one could also go on imaginary journeys. The shelter had only three walls; the front was entirely open. Under its roof stood the family carriage and a row of carts and wagons of assorted sizes, looking quite inane with their shafts resting on the earthern floor. It was amusing to climb to the highest seats and pretend you were riding off somewhere. You could sit in the two-seated carriage, give the reins a tug, and be on your way to church in Colijnsplaat, all dressed in your best clothes and fragrant with cologne. Or you could mount the big wide open seat of the longest wagon there and drive a load of hay in from the fields. There seemed no end to the possibilities.

When coffee time came at mid-morning the girls pranced into the kitchen for a babelaar while Adriaan sat at the table sipping hot cupfuls and eating slices of bread and butter. When Adriaan, Jr. was home he joined his father at the table.

Elizabeth, who was tutored at home, was eleven when a second son, Jacobus, was born to the De Prees. From that time on Neeltje spent a little more time in the house, helping with small tasks. Her visits usually came to an end on a Sunday morning, when the family drove into town to church. At about half past eight, while Moe Betje in her Brussels lace cap and brown silk blouse tucked her snuf doosje into her sak and ran an eye over Elizabeth and Neeltje, Adriaan hitched the small brown mare Meisje (Girl) to the carriage and drove up to the house. The surrey had been dusted and cleaned on Saturday; Betje could safely entrust her black cashmere skirt to the patent leather seat.

Riding into town those memorable Sunday mornings when a visit was coming to an end, Neeltje, her play clothes in a bundle at her feet, would be filled with contentment. She'd had a good time, and now she looked forward to seeing her family and living in the house beside the sea, where in the evening the beacon at Brouwershaven sent its cone of light through the darkness, and earlier, at sundown, the far reaches of water and the immense sky were luminous with gold.

Slanted Pockets

Jan walked on air the day his father took him to the tailor's to be measured for his new suit. He had finally reached his eighth birthday and so earned the right to wear clothes like his father's. Up to that time he had worn the dark blouses and knee-length black pants common to all the island boys, and a small black beret.

Then came the day when the order was ready and brought home. Jan up in his room put on his new outfit, then went down and strolled over to the city hall walk, where the skippers in port stood about smoking and talking. His tan cap was a jaunty affair with a stubby visor, and his short buttoned jacket and long pants, slightly flared at the ankle, gave him a new air. They were made of a light silver-brown bombazine, a felt-like wool that became soft as sealskin after some wearing. In front of the *Stadhuis* he stood among the men, listening to their talk and feeling like one of them, his hands thrust deep into his generous pockets. He felt inches taller, suddenly, and he was jubilant with pride.

His wooden shoes were in seamen's style, coming to a point at the toe. Landlubbers, he reflected complacently, wore square-toed shoes. They had no visors on their caps, and they wore black trousers whose pockets at the opening ran parallel to the seam. The skipper's pockets were cut on an oblique line. Jan and all the young skipper crowd were alert to these points of difference; their pride in their link with the sea was so great that if the son of a landsman came out in a pair of pointed shoes or in trousers with slanted pockets, they would see to it that he'd think twice before doing so again.

On Sundays, now, when Jan had to lay aside the new brown costume and put on his black dress suit and cap, his elation went on undiminished; for he had said goodbye to the women's section at the church and was at long last sitting beside Adriaan and Marinus in their father's pew, over on the south side of the sanctuary where most of the skippers sat.

A boy wearing seaman-style clothes. Origin unknown.

A Braid to Reckon With

When Jan's sister Leun was a slip of a girl with a thick crop of short dark hair she had the nickname of "Pruik," or Wig. She was the impetuous one in the family, seldom inside when she could be out-of-doors. From morning to night she was on the move and there seemed no limit to her energy or appetite. Maria, sandy-haired and blue-eyed, was Leun's understudy and attached herself to her as soon as she was able to run and keep up with her.

In school as everywhere else Leun's exuberance led her into difficulties. It was a weariness to Lavina to see her high-spirited daughter sitting over her slate in the evening writing her one hundred lines; and she made no secret of her displeasure. Finally Leun, dreading her mother's reproofs more than the boredom of her assignment, considered her resources and changed her program. Now when she took her slate home she tucked it quickly away in some inconspicuous spot and left it there until she was ready to leave the house the next morning.

By eating her breakfast a little more swiftly and hurrying out earlier than usual she found time to stop in at her Uncle David's carpenter shop on the Voorstraat. There, sitting on a nail keg or a stack of lumber in the corner, she scratched away with her griffel.

Ik ben een ondeugende meid.
Ik ben een ondeugende meid.
Ik ben een ondeugende meid.

The more often she wrote the line (I am a disobedient girl.) the more convinced she became of the truth of the words and the more easily she continued being een ondeugende meid. It was a vicious circle. But she consoled herself with the thought that at least she was getting good practice in writing. Lavina, no longer seeing the slate and pencil, assumed that her child was improving; and Leun's blithe outlook went on undisturbed.

As "Pruik" grew older and her interest in her appearance increased she let her thick hair grow. The result was a heavy, luxuriant braid—the longest and heaviest, she was sure, in the entire village. It was her pride, and she knew how to use it as a psychological weapon. Like the other girls of her age she kept it tied with a bright ribbon. Whenever she had a quarrel or an argument with one of her friends she would bring her hair around and retie the bow, then with a proud toss of her head and a flip of her hand swing the braid back over her shoulder in a wide, conspicuous arc. If her opponent's eyes sharpened with envy or chagrin the spirited Leun knew that she had triumphed.

Legend and Song

In the house on the Achterstraat where Jan's grandparents Marinus and Adriana lived, the front room was a little store. On one side oil and fish and pork were sold and on the other, groceries. When on weekdays the bell on the door jangled, a windowed door at the rear of the store opened and Adriana stepped in to greet her customer.

Sometimes it was one of her grandchildren whose coming rang the bell, most likely Leun, to whom the little shop was an oversized cupboard, tantalizing with dried fruits, among other things, and sweets. But the rooms beyond the store were a greater attraction; here Leun often came with her cousin Jaantje Karreman to while away an afternoon with their grandmother.

The glass door led into a broad room with a hearth in the center of the opposite wall and on each side of the hearth a window looking out on the bleaching green, the barn, and the carpenter shop. This was the shop where Jan came with discarded wooden shoes to be made into boats, and cherry pits to be ground on the big grindstone. At the base of the windows were wide, deep sills, and under the sills built-in shelves where the grandfather kept his rows of books, each wrapped in a jacket of yellow paper treated with oil. Marinus Merizon was a native of France, but he had lived in the Netherlands since he was four. His parents had lost their lives in the religious persecutions, and refugees brought the young boy to Holland. He grew up faithful to his heritage and was well grounded in the tenets of his faith. Many of those books on his shelves were church history and theological works.

Against the right-hand wall of the pleasant room stood the tall cabinet, its polished wood rich with the patina of years, and across from it the buffet. Built-in beds flanked the door, and in the center of the room a round table stood on a rug that covered most of the floor. Under the rug lay a matting that reached to the walls. It was into this room, where on chilly days a peat fire glowed and whispered on the hearth and the walnut surfaces gleamed with a satin light, that Leun came with her cousin.

A stranger coming upon Adriana in repose might have judged from the soft look in her grey eyes that she was essentially shy; but her speech was forthright and free, and when she rose and moved about, her erect carriage and the set of her head on her shoulders would soon have dispelled the earlier impression.

Her crisp white cap and the gold krullen at her temples were in bright contrast to her dark, smooth hair. She usually wore a black full skirt and a jacket of some becoming color with a pleated peplum at her small waist. A shawl of sheer silk was draped around her shoulders and tucked in soft folds into the deep oval neckline. Leun and Jaantje admired her artful way of dressing, and Leun could not help contrasting it with her other, more sober, grandmother's plain attire.

Adriana seated the girls before the fire and drew them out with questions. If it was a Sunday afternoon she would ask, "Did you go to the *knicker kerk* with your other grandmother this morning?" Knicker meant something so small that a good-size marble would look enormous beside it! And that was her mischievous way of reminding the girls that their grandfather Marinus was a member of the State Church, the "Groote Kerk," as it was commonly called. She probably surmised that Leun mentioned her name for the church on the Achterweg to grandmother Betje Breas, and took pleasure in the thought. For Adriana and Betje were poles apart, and no one knew it better than they. Betje's home was only a stone's throw distant, but the two women might have been living on opposite sides of the island. Years passed, sometimes, without their meeting or exchanging a word.

Those Sunday afternoons the two girls always came with the hope that Grootmoeder would make a batch of *babelaars* for them; and they were seldom disappointed. Out in the kitchen they watched as she tumbled a heap of brown sugar into an iron kettle, then added a little water and vinegar, a pinch of salt, and a lump of butter. Back in the living room she hung the kettle over the fire, and the three took their chairs and sat comfortably around the hearth.

In her many years of making babelaars Adriana had developed a good sense of timing. When the candy was about ready she dipped a long iron spoon into the pot and raised it aloft; if it sent out a fluff of fine-spun filaments she lifted the kettle from the hook and poured the transparent brown mass onto a buttered platter. It was said that too much pulling took some of the sweetness out of the candy; so Adriana let it cool until it was fairly stiff. Then, working at the round table covered with oilcloth, she pulled the mass into long ropes and chopped off small pillow-shaped pieces. When she finished she had a good, generous dishful. For the next hour it was babelaars unlimited, and Jaantje and Leun ate their blissful fill. But Adriana discreetly arranged to have all signs of candy-making out of sight before her husband returned from afternoon worship, for he was far more conscientious than she was about keeping the Sabbath day holy and avoiding unnecessary work.

Sometimes the girls were able to persuade Grootmoeder to tell them stories, and her tales gave them even greater pleasure than the babelaars. She could make their eyes fly wide open and stand out in their heads. She believed in warnings. Many a time it has happened, so she said, that a man while going about his work has suddenly felt a tap on his shoulder. Looking about and seeing no one, he realized what had happened and was stunned; for he knew that his fate was sealed. He must soon die. And always the warning was borne out in fact. He died.

Leun would breathe a deep sigh and help herself to another babelaar. The sweetness of the candy on her tongue and the chill of the words in her ear were a combination to keep her enrapt. She could have sat for hours.

Adriana had ways of varying her entertainment. Sometimes when a tale was completed she would break off from her tellings and go over to the cabinet, step up on a chair, and from the top shelf bring down the box containing her jewels. Though she still wore her gold krullen at her temples she had long ago put away the pendant bellen and spiral spellen as suitable only for younger women. These she took out and handed to the girls to examine and admire. Then there were the necklaces—six- and eight-strand chokers of bright coral and of deep-red garnets fitted with wide golden clasps; and brooches elaborately molded and studded with semiprecious stones. The young guests handled them with care and respect, delighting in their brilliance and sheen and their voluptuous weight. Serenely they assumed that when they reached the age for putting up their hair they too would wear the traditional gold, just as their grandmother had when she was young.

There were times when Adriana was in a mood for song, and when the stories had been told or the jewels put away she would begin to sing—old, sad love songs and ballads full of longing and despair. As she sang she would move her head and flash her eyes expressively, and no prima donna ever enthralled an audience more completely than Adriana did hers. The two young girls sat spellbound, their hearts torn almost out of them in sympathy for the distraught lovers.

So the afternoon flew. Before they knew it *Grootvader* was walking in and daylight had faded. The bewitching bubble of legend and romance they had lived in for an afternoon dissolved. After a few words with the grandfather they put on their coats, promised to come again soon, and hurried home to supper.

A Winter Kitchen

In all the kitchens of Colijnsplaat a bench stood behind the table where the family took their meals. It held a row of children and saved a good amount of chair space. The bench in Lavina's kitchen in the house that faced the dike had to be short, for the table was a round one. It was covered with oilcloth held down around the edge with a strip of wood like a barrel hoop. On a wall shelf stood the eight-day clock, and beside the clock lay the Bible and a few other books the skipper liked to have near at hand. The cupboards, the peat-burning range, and a bench holding a basin, a pail of water, and a dipper completed the kitchen furnishings.

During the spring, summer, and fall this room, a one-story extension at the back of the house, was the center of all activity; but before winter gales swooped down on the village the kitchen was drawn in under the main roof, like a turtle's head drawn in when protection is needed. Out of the living room were carried the polished chairs and table and the wool rug, and into it went a rush matting for the floor, the big round table, the bench, and the kitchen chairs. Here all through the winter the family spent their waking hours.

The hearth that in spring and fall held open fires was hidden, now, behind a half-moon stove that both heated the room and provided a surface for cooking. Every Friday, when the whole village was taken with a frenzy of cleaning and scrubbing, the fire was allowed to die out so that the stove could be blackened and burnished and its nickel made to glitter like glass. The children came home from school those Friday afternoons to a bleak, cold kitchen, but by supper time a fire danced once more in the black cage, flooding the room with cheer.

Meals were always bustling affairs, with eleven hungry ones circling the table. At noon there would be a heaping dish of white, crumbly potatoes, a platter of pork or fish, and sauerkraut or green beans from a deep crock of brine.

One of Lavina's treasures, familiar to the children and as much a part of the house as the table and chairs, was the tea caddy of blue china with its hammered brass top. When she lifted the lid there floated through the room the aroma of choice teas from Java and Sumatra. She brewed a generous pot and poured cups for all the children as well as for herself and Adriaan.

Sitting inconspicuously in the wide circle, Jan would be preoccupied with his own thoughts, bringing to the table, among other things, his passion for ships. After he had mashed his potatoes and patted them down flat on his plate he would carve out a hull, a mast, and sails, and eat first the extraneous potato around the edge of the silhouette. When the ship had to go he ate a sail, then another, then the mast, and finally, inevitably, the hull.

There was little time to linger after the noon dinner; but at supper time a sense of leisure held the family longer around the table. The skipper said little during the meal; like all Dutch *burghers,* he preferred to concentrate on his food. But when the last drop of coffee had been drained from his cup and he had read aloud from the Scriptures and returned thanks, he would often stay at the table with the children and tell them stories from the Old Testament. Like his mother, Adriana, he was a gifted narrator; and Daniel and David, Esther and others of the great figures became vivid and real to his listeners. The skipper's eyes shone with his Huguenot faith and he was alive in every nerve as he recounted for the sacred histories, for he longed to share with his children the certainties that were the center of his life.

With the first softening of winter's edge and the faint, early heraldings of spring on the moist sea air, Lavina was taken with a desire to put her house in order. The big oilcloth-covered table, the bench, and the chairs were carried back to the kitchen, the stove was dismantled and put away, and the living room stood empty. Then the rug was aired and beaten and proudly spread, and the mahogany chairs and table, gleaming with a new coat of wax, were restored to their places. And when at last the room stood complete and inviting, it was like a far retreat, out of the path of the ceaseless daily traffic—a small area of elegance and privacy for those special hours that mean so much to the members of a bubbling household.

No one would have dreamed, to look at it now, that it was the same room that had housed so much homely activity throughout the winter months.

Saltwater and Sweet

It was on an evening in late winter, while the family was still using the winter kitchen, that Maria, who was eight or nine at the time, had one of the big surprises of her young life. Vader was away on a trip to Rotterdam.

Beginning to clear the table while the children sat lingering and talking, Lavina gave Maria the syrup pitcher to carry to the summer kitchen. The long hall leading to the back of the house was dark, but Maria knew the way and sped through the gloom on confident feet. Suddenly, however, there was nothing to step on, and in terror she was falling into a hole and floundering in a pool of icy water. In the cozy room above the family heard a splash and a cry. The trap door! Someone had left it open! But before anyone could run to Maria's help she had flown up the ladder quick as a cat and stood shivering in their presence.

Shock and anxiety and relief struck Lavina in such quick succession that for the moment she was dumb. But relief soon won out, for here stood Maria before her, miserable but safe and apparently unharmed, and looking so funny that one just had to laugh. With Moeder in the lead the room broke into merriment.

Presently Lavina was all mother again. Was Maria all right? Where were her shoes? And the syrup? She comforted the child and promised dry clothes immediately. Then taking the lantern she peered down the trap hole to the dark pool below. There two wooden shoes floated as serenely as boats on a canal; the syrup pitcher had of course gone to the bottom. Adriaan must go down the ladder with a stick and fish out those klompen. "Now be careful, Adriaan, and close the trap door the minute you come up. And the rest of you stay right here in this room. Come, Maria."

A cellar half full of water was common in winter. In summer there might be less, but always there was water. The island was like a sponge, drenched by the sea and the river. In summertime a part of its moisture was lifted into the air through the grass, the crops, and the leafy-crowned trees, but in winter it lay locked below the surface.

All this water provided not a drop to fill a cup for thirsty children, however, or to brew a fragrant pot of tea. The only source of drinking water on the island was the rain that ran down the red tile roofs to the cisterns. On the farms and in all the villages the rain was caught and channeled and stored, its availability as much a life-and-death matter as the shutting out of the tons of saltwater that beat against the dikes.

In the skipper's house the cistern holding the rainwater was sunk below the kitchen floor. A box-like enclosure against the wall and a closefitting lid kept the small children safe from its hazards, but the older ones liked to peer into its eerie depths and hear their voices ring in the cavern above the water. The snails clinging to its concrete wall and those that came up in the pail were looked upon as allies. They were said to keep the water pure.

But the rains did not supply all the water needed for the household. Water for washing and cleaning was drawn from a well out in the yard. It straddled the boundary line between two lots and was shared with Mijnheer Beune, the schoolmaster. There was little visiting at the well, however, for the tall, solid board fence separating the backyards, and the fence-like enclosure at the mouth of the well, were a barrier to easy conversation between neighbors.

Once in a great while, when rains were far apart, though the island continued green as an emerald the cistern in the kitchen would echo like a hollow shell, and Adriaan would shake his head over the length of rope he had to drop before the pail hit the water. The family was warned to go sparingly with the dipper until showers replenished the supply. At length the day came when Lavina would have to send Neeltje and Leun or two other children with a pail to a house on the Dorpstraat near the school, where a

Woman carrying pails, sketch by Armand Merizon

woman who managed to catch more rain than others sold the precious liquid at a penny and a half or two cents a pail.

Coming home, no matter how much they wanted to hurry and be free, the two young carriers restrained themselves and watched their load. Spilling would only mean another tiresome trip that much sooner. And besides, they had learned to respect and appreciate these drops from the sky. They had tasted the water from the well and it had puckered their mouths. They would rather go thirsty then drink such bitter brine! And besides, Vader said it wouldn't be good for them.

Home Over the Roofs

At the corner of the Achterstraat and the Dorpstraat stood a house somewhat longer than most of those in the neighborhood. The front room was used as a store, the central part was living quarters, and the rear was a stockroom and retail center quite unrelated to the little shop at the front.

The store facing the street was a dry goods shop, where Dena Koole, the plump, kindhearted mother of five boys, would hustle out to wait on a customer, linger for some neighborly talk, then hurry back to take up her housework where she had left off. It was an unpretentious little shop, supplying thread and needles and yard goods for making everyday clothes and household linens. Those who wanted beautiful fabrics and exquisite laces went to Middelburg or had someone shop for them while there.

Dena's husband, Peter, who was a skipper with a route to Antwerp, brought in all the coal that was burned in the stoves and hearths of Colijnsplaat and sold it from the large shed at the rear of his house. The villagers came with wheelbarrows, entering the storeroom from the Dorpstraat and trundling their coal away in burlap sacks.

Often when Peter was away on a voyage good-hearted Dena would allow customers to take coal out on credit. When her husband returned he shook his head over her easy ways, and before many days had passed he went out on an evening after dark and collected his accounts. The burlap sacks were supposed to be returned to him, but often when knocking at a door he found himself wiping his feet on one! They were too much of a temptation to the thrifty housewives; they washed the black dust out, dried them smooth, and laid them down for doormats.

Len, the oldest of the five Koole boys, was the resourceful leader of the skipper crowd, and everyone was conscious of him, including Cornelisse, the village policeman. Len wore gold earrings, like a pirate, and these together with his great verve and his instinct for pranks gave small girls like Jo and Margrieta the impression that he was a terror. They stayed as far from him as they could.

Summer days were long on the North Sea, but late in the season when darkness began to close in earlier the boys would still be out when twilight fell. This was the time of year when the sea was most often strange and beautiful with phosphorescence. The water where disturbed was like burning liquid, and ships had foam like fire at their prows. When the sea was in this exciting state the boys were too fascinated to leave the pier. By some happy concurrence of nature this was also the time when the new harvest of sugar beets lay piled on the quay ready to be put into the holds of ships. In so lavish a cargo a few beets more or less

Boys playing at seashore. Origin unknown.

made little difference, and helping themselves from the generous piles the boys skipped the beets over the water and watched the leaping, fiery spray.

But amusement did not always come so easily or with so guileless a face.

Saturday was a full day for the housewives of the village, for in their endeavor to obey the fourth commandment they prepared ahead for their Sunday needs. Late in the day they peeled a big kettle of potatoes, covered them with cold water, and from some long-established custom set them on the floor in the long hall to await the dinner hour next day. Suddenly some Saturday evening a weary mother would hear a thud and a sprawling of water, and going out to investigate she would find her kettle overturned. At the same time there would be a rush of shadowy figures down the street and around the corner.

One night when something like this had been going on Cornelisse went over to the Koole house, planted himself at the corner where he could watch both doors, and waited. But he had done this before. Darkness fell and the crowd was breaking up. Len, peering down the street and seeing a certain forbidding figure standing near his home, took off his klompen and tied them on a strip of rope he had in his pocket. With the rope slung around his neck he climbed up a nearby house and crawled hand-over-hand up and down the angled roofs to his own home, where his brothers had an upstairs window open for him. Without a sound and with the litheness of a cat Len dropped safely to the ledge and eased himself into the room.

It was a great joke, and the boys, giggling, hurried to a window where they could look down on Cornelisse, standing there so officially.

"Wasn't it good though," they chuckled, wondering how long the officer would stand there.

A Door Swings Open

Out at High Meadow—the home that held Jo's earliest memories—her uncle Willem De Jonge and his family thrived on the farm. But now an unseen enemy was invading those fertile fields. It was a day in full summer when Pieternella, Jo's cousin, saw her father come into the kitchen carrying a basket of freshly dug potatoes. He seemed preoccupied and began immediately to examine the potatoes one by one, saying quietly as he did so, "This one has it. This one has it. This one..." Questioning him, Pieternella learned that a disease affecting most of the farms in the area was causing the potatoes to rot in the ground. Very likely their crop would be a total loss.

The loss was a blow to Willem, for he depended on the crop for a good part of his income. Besides, he would have to go out and buy a supply for his own table, and that meant a considerable outlay, for they were a family of ten. The kettle that held the potatoes to be cooked was wide and deep, and every day Wilhelmina peeled and peeled until it was filled almost to the brim.

But the blight on the potatoes was only the beginning of many troubles. In the years that followed the weather was unfavorable for crops, and a general depression settled over the land. Jan and Elizabeth De Jonge were caught in the lull along with everyone else; but for some time now, while Willem and other folk had still enjoyed prosperity, they had been finding the going more and more difficult. It was Jan's temperament and personality, so some of his kinsmen claimed, that lay at the bottom of his difficulties. Jan's talents were social and creative, so they said; he hadn't a practical hair on his head. A genial host, he kept in his living room a rack of special pipes inscribed with the names of his friends and the members of the consistory, which sometimes met in his home. Here on an evening with a good friend or two, their pipes drawing well and their minds playing around a subject of common interest, Jan was in his element.

But in matters of business on the farm he was idealistic and naive, and his impulsive and sympathetic nature led him into too many generosities and enterprises. Elizabeth, who was accustomed to a modest plentitude, was forced to practice increasing frugality. Like all good European cooks she had a generous hand with the butter; but now with the cattle sold she had to watch herself. She mended with infinite patience the linens and clothing and was careful to send the shoes to the schoenmakker before they were worn beyond repair.

At length she and Jan faced the blow that had been threatening them. They arranged to sell their house and the big new barn. The two sat silently together one day,

Elizabeth in her white cap and gingham apron and Jan in a dark waistcoat, brooding over their impending loss and feeling utterly disheartened, when Jo, happy and unaware, burst into the room. She had just come from one of the little shops and held in her hands a penny's worth of English walnuts. Quickly sensing their dejection, she offered them two of the three blond-shelled nuts. But they shook their heads, murmuring that she should eat and enjoy them; and their faces remained sad. Bewildered, Jo left the room and slipped out at the front door.

The Volunteer Fire Brigade was out on a practice alarm. Adriaan Vande Wiele, Chief of the Lantern Carriers, hurried along, lantern in hand, rehearsing for some possible emergency in the night—though fires at any hour were as rare in Colijnsplaat as robbers. Through the streets and out to the pond the brigade rushed, a bevy of men pulling by a long rope the pump and hose on four wheels. Jo joined other children as they followed the procession on flying feet and clustered around while the pumping men bent and rose in perfect rhythm and the hose played a stream of water on imaginary flames. To Jo and to all the young it was a splendid performance, and as she stood watching, the walnuts in her hand were forgotten and the sorrow of her mother and father was as though it never had been.

Moving day came, and evening found the De Jonges settling down in a house on the New Mill Way. Elizabeth ached with fatigue and lethargy, while her children, to whom one house was as good as another, skipped in and out enjoying the novelty of a new location.

But even this retrenchment did not help for long. Jan's anxieties increased as time went on. There were seven children when they left their house on the Achterstraat. After Johannes, the first boy, two more girls had come—Mariena and, two years later, Neeltje, who was named for the little girl who had died. Now, in their home on the New Mill Way, Gerard, their ninth and last child, was born. Casting about for a firm footing, Jan found himself entertaining more and more what seemed at the time a stupendous and daring idea. Why not go to "Amerika"! Every week, or with every sailing, so it seemed, people from the Province were leaving on the long voyage westward.

Elizabeth turned away from the thought when first it was suggested to her. Put the ocean between her and her people? How could she do it! She had been the youngest child in her family and orphaned while still a young girl. Her attachment to her brothers and sisters and their children was one that had grown out of dependence as well as affection. To sail away and leave them, perhaps never to see them again, would be like tearing her heart in two and leaving a part of herself behind. But Jan was not deterred. He returned to the idea again and again, and the more he thought about going the more convinced he felt that it was the thing to do.

Once more it became necessary for the De Jonges to move; this time they took a house facing the moat along its eastern side. But their fortunes in Colijnsplaat were no longer of final significance to them. Elizabeth knew all too well the necessity of a change, and though she still found the idea depressing and difficult to face, she saw the prospect of new beginnings and a more spacious future for their children as a gift held out irresistibly in an open hand.

Even Willem was toying with the thought of going to America. He who had felt so rooted in his farm and expected to finish his days there was caught under the spell of his brother's scheme. He knew that of course the years of poor crops were only a small arc in a broad cycle, that conditions would improve and his fields give again their normal and generous yield. But the urge grew. The thought of great sweeps of land and growing towns and cities appealed to him as nothing familiar ever could again; and after long conversations with their wives he and Jan decided to write to their cousins in America.

Once their letter was posted the matter was settled. Already a change had taken place in their lives, and they hid as best they could their inner excitement.

The friends Elizabeth confided in joked with her now about those rocking chairs they had heard were so common in America. Perhaps she too would soon be spending her afternoons rocking. They envisioned them as something outlandish but at the same time pleasurable, a symbol of the ease and luxury to be found in that never-neverland across the sea.

Weeks went by, and finally one day Jan found waiting for him at the post office a letter bearing strange stamps and a foreign postmark. Home in a hurry and reading the letter aloud to Elizabeth, he found all the encouragement he had hoped for. Jan and his family were invited to stay with his cousin Francois Lucasse, and Willem, Wilhelmina, and their children were to go to Francois's brother Marinus. The two Lucasses lived in Kalamazoo, a city in southwest Michigan.

With little delay Jan walked to the farm to carry the news to Willem. As the two brothers stood in the yard trying to take in the implications of what they were planning they looked down at the native soil under their feet and then away into the distance. It seemed almost unbelievable. But it was all in the providence of God; of that they were sure.

Now the talking and planning went forward in earnest. Wilhelmina and Elizabeth began making lists of the things they would sell and those they would take with them. And the men went off on a most important trip to South Beveland. There at the office of the steamship company they entered their names on the waiting list for passage to America.

Farewell, Tannetje!

It was on a pleasant evening in August, in the year 1887, that Jan and Elizabeth stood in the wide hall of their stripped, echoing house, bidding goodby those who had come for final farewells. The children gathered round the doorstep, the little girls in yellow pinafores that their cousin had made especially for their voyage. They found it impossible to sit still or stand in one spot for any length of time. In spite of the attention they were receiving from aunts and uncles, cousins and friends, they were filled with eagerness to be on their way.

The families were to sail as far as Rotterdam with Skipper Merizon, leaving Colijnsplaat with the midnight tide. Now as the sun dipped low in the west and long shadows lay upon the streets, Jan and Elizabeth closed the door behind them for the last time and with their excited brood and a host of company took a leisurely walk to the harbor. The last sunlight of the day lay on the water as they went aboard.

Never in Adriaan's memory had the small boat carried so many passengers. Besides Jan and Elizabeth's family there were Willem and Wilhelmina De Jonge with six boys and two girls and Willem's hired man, Jan Legerste, a widower with two small sons and a daughter. Tannetje would accompany them to Rotterdam as she had promised; and Lavina Merizon would go as hostess on her husband's boat.

As long as they lingered in the harbor and the long northern twilight held back the night there were many who clung to the presence of the emigrating families. Friends and kin stood on the quay and talked back and forth with those on deck, heartening them for their journey and reminding them to send letters promptly.

With her sisters and brother Johannes and the other children, Jo wandered contentedly about, luxuriating in all the new sensations of being on board. The nearness of the water thrilled her, and the sails and yards, the anchor wench, the hatch, and the water cask with its brass drinking cup and chain were all part of the boat world that although so near had never before been freely available to her.

It had long been a source of injured pride to Jo that Margrieta had had the experience of sailing, while she had not. Their father had once taken Margrieta to visit an aunt in Goes, South Beveland, choosing her to go because she was her aunt's namesake. Jannetje and Jo had watched them off with hearts full of rebellion; what if Margrieta was named after their tante; weren't they older than she? But Margrieta had gone, and when she returned she was filled with the pleasures of the ferry ride and the coveted visit. Now at last Jo's injured pride was to be healed, for the coming voyage would carry them all so far and last so long that the little trip to South Beveland would be as nothing.

Jo leaned against the gunwhale, lost in reverie, and noticed that a stick that was partially submerged appeared to bend abruptly at the water line. This puzzled and intrigued her, and she was wishing to lift the stick and find out whether it really was bent or whether it only appeared to be, when suddenly her name was called and she ran to join her sisters disappearing one by one into the hold. The children were gleeful as they scrambled down the flat-runged ladder. Going upstairs to bed was an old routine; going down a ladder to an improvised encampment in a boat was a lark.

On tarpaulins stretched on the floor Wilhelmina and Elizabeth had spread their feather beds, taken temporarily from packing cases. Side by side in billowy rows the soft, inviting things now lay, and after the commotion of preparations amid a buzz of chatter the nineteen children were assigned to their places, covered with wool blankets, and told to be quiet and go to sleep. Where would they find themselves in the morning? They would have to wait and see, but it would be far from Colijnsplaat—far away.

The evening light faded, and on Schouwen and Tholen the great beacons burned. At about eleven o'clock the skipper hoisted one of the foresails; immediately the sea wind caught it, filled it, and carried the boat gently away from the quay. The passengers on deck called goodby to those who had waited to see them off in the darkness, and then the boat left the sheltered waters of the harbor and entered the broad estuary. More sail was hoisted, and Colijnsplaat, almost invisible now behind the harbor lights, fell rapidly away.

Next morning when the children clambered up to the deck they found all the wonderful panorama of Dordrecht lying to starboard. Such a succession of windmills, boats, barges, and houses of every shape, size, and color! And everywhere people moving about. Their eyes could not take it in fast enough—so much there was to see.

From then on, all the way to Rotterdam, the sights along the shores kept them curious and alert. As they neared the great seaport and steam trams began to appear among the medley of masts and buildings, Jo several times spied one of them coming their way. She would be all expectation, hoping it would continue its course and pass close by. But invariably the tram turned away from the river before it came near their boat. Each time this happened her hopes collapsed, like a bird in mid-air suddenly shorn of its wings, and she would stand and watch helplessly while the tantalizing thing veered and rolled farther and farther away.

Elizabeth, busy with small Gerard and Neeltje and enjoying the last days of Tannetje's presence, was much less aware of the colorful world they were gliding through. Her preoccupations were all with the future that awaited her and Jan and the children. There were presentiments, too, of the pain she would feel in the months and years to come, when her island and her people were no longer within sight or touch or hearing.

But one could not be altogether pensive with Lavina around. A realist to the core, she looked on this venture with a practical cheerfulness, and her warm, infectious humor bubbled up and leavened her firm command as she dealt with every small emergency.

Elizabeth had taken along the few things that meant most to the family, so that in the home they would establish in America they would have here and there objects familiar to their eyes and hands—intimate, material things that would nevertheless be almost like living friends in the midst of that strange new world. Into the big cases and trunks she had packed all their clothes, many of which had been made in the house beside the mill, and their feather beds and blankets. Her linens and silver were included, and a few personal possessions—her jewelry and that of her daughters, her snuf doosje and pepermunt doosje, and the family Bible with its golden clasps. Jan saw to it that his *varrekieker,* or hand telescope, came along and the best of his favorite books, among them his *Brakel.* And lest the food on the *Leerdam* during their crossing be not altogether familiar and to their liking, Elizabeth had arranged to take on board, along with her teapot, a great supply of cinnamon rolls, fresh from her baker's that last day, and her favorite deep earthenware crock filled with butter!

The small boat with its lively cargo sailed steadily on, a seasoned voyager in the thickening traffic, and in good time nosed into her berth in the Haringvliet Quay. Since the *Leerdam* would not be sailing until the following day the carefree young of the party went off with the men on sightseeing trips in the city. On their return they gave the women graphic and excited accounts of all that they had seen.

It was decided that for their final meal together the *Lavina's* passengers would have a gala fish dinner. Such quantities of flounder as were bought and prepared! They required more than the two frying pans the galley provided; so Adriaan Jr., the skipper's mate, was sent off to buy another. Meanwhile the women peeled the choice, purple-skinned potatoes that had been kept especially for the feast—*blauwe jannen,* they were called, or "blue johns"—and set the table in the hold, a table of banquet proportions improvised from sawhorses and wooden planks.

It was a dinner to be remembered ever after: the delicate-flavored fish fried in butter, accompanied by mounds of snowy potatoes topped with rich, yellow butter gravy; the long table seating twenty-eight, on a small boat anchored in a harbor thronging with the commerce of the world; and within certain members of the party the poignant awareness of being together for perhaps the last time.

Lavina and the skipper with Tannetje and Adriaan, Jr. stood on the dock beside the *Leerdam,* lifting their hands in a last goodby. When finally they walked away it was with feelings of reluctance and regret, but withal a sense of elation for those who were departing. Tannetje turned again and again to wave once more to the row of silhouettes along the rail, while Adriaan, Jr., his hands in his pockets, kept his course straight ahead and his thoughts and feelings to himself. For it was of blond, blue-eyed Pieternella, Willem's daughter, that he was thinking, and he lamented romantically within himself that this, alas, was the end.

Up on the deck Jo, watching Tannetje walk away and grow smaller and less discernible among the crowds in the distance, felt a new, strange sensation of loneliness. Tannetje! She wanted to call her back—to beg her to go with them to America.

Once when Jo as a very small child had burned herself badly tipping a hot kettle down toward her, Tannetje had held her comfortingly and stroked the smarting wound with the tip of a feather dipped in oil. It had felt like the softest feather in the world. Jo was never to forget that ministration, and although now as she stood watching her cousin walk away her childish thoughts were not of the things Tannetje had done, still her feeling of dependence and sudden deprivation was a result of all that the warm, spontaneous girl had come to mean to her and to the family.

Surprisingly for the children, the *Leerdam* did not sail away promptly after they went aboard. Impatient and disappointed, they finally gave up and began exploring the ship. It seemed to them of tremendous size, and its maze of passageways and staterooms was bewildering after the simplicity of the little boat from Colijnsplaat.

At long last they began to move, and when finally after slow maneuverings the *Leerdam* left the harbor and river behind and plowed full speed through open water, they looked down on the foam tossed from its prow and the deep troughs in its wake and marveled that they were riding so mighty a ship.

Jan and Elizabeth with Willem, Wilhelmina and Jan Legerste watched the retreating shore until "Nederland" was only a vague line on the horizon. And then the line faded and was gone, and the sea alone lay all around.

But "Amerika" lay ahead.

TANNETJE SENDS A LETTER

The Potappel Mill
Colijnsplaat, N.B.

Dearest Uncle and Aunt, and dear Nieces and Nephews:

Since Tante was so brave a traveler I dare not put off writing any longer. Forgive me please that I did not write you earlier, but when Father wrote I was busy sewing and getting ready to go to s'Heer Arendskerke....Sometimes the pen is as heavy for me as the mast of the Leerdam, *so that I cannot think of writing; and then too we have been so constantly busy, if not sewing then visiting. Joppa was home for eight days, and whenever I'd talk about our trip to Rotterdam she would sit with her mouth open, and we laughed sometimes till the tears ran down our cheeks—especially when I imitated cousin Lavina! I say so often, she was like a* hussar, met haar stads mode.[4]

O Tante, how quiet and empty it was when we went aboard after we had taken you all to the ship! Adriaan Merizon cried, 'But those poor people—what they will have to overcome!' He also said he wouldn't care to start out for America with so little money. But cousin Lavina said, 'Don't say that. We might wish that we too were on our way there, even if we shouldn't have a cent left when we arrived in America.'

She might wish that they were there, for now they are dead poor, and then would cousin Viena perhaps already be sitting in a rocking chair. She would not say 'No thank you,' as you did. Neeltje and I laughed so hard as we read that, for we would like to rock and rock too, so that we would end up in the corner of the room!

Tante, if you or the children write, tell us how your jacket is,

---

[5] met haar stads mode: with her big-city air.

Tannetje Potappel

and if that dear Gerard walks alone now, for we are so much interested in him. A. Boot said that your children all look so healthy; that is not true of us, for we are all having colds and Cornelia is very weak. She talks so much about you, especially when she has clothes that are getting too small; then she often says, 'Now if Neeltje were not in America she could wear these very nicely.'

It is now eleven o'clock, and all are sleeping except Pietje, Neeltje, and I. Pietje is sewing on the machine and so I can hardly write. She is planning to go on a trip to Yerseke, where Willem lives.

And now Tante I must close; I have no more news. But when you meet our dear old neighbors give our greetings, especially mine. The picture is for Jo. She will know about it for I promised her but forgot to give it.

May you receive these words in the best of health. So I remain with all regard and affection,

Your loving niece,

Tannetje

(Translated from Dutch)

The Advance Guard

It was not only fathers and mothers, weary with the strain of long anxiety, who turned hopefully to the west in those years of slow returns. The young, too, were touched by the fever.

While the winds of autumn blew upon the house that faced the dike Elizabeth and Leun, having heard compelling things about the land across the sea, put their pretty heads together and wrote a letter of some import to their uncle in America.

When their grandmother Elizabeth Breas had lost her husband years before and was left a young widow with six dependent children, her brother-in-law, Jasper Breas, stood by to help her; and when her two sons Jasper and Peter finished public school he provided for their further education in South Holland. Their mother was grateful for all this; but to her dismay their years away at school extended their horizons beyond her expectations, and on completing their courses they sailed away to other continents. Jasper, the oldest son, went to the United States, and Peter accepted a position with the Dutch government in Paramaribo, Dutch Guiana.

Years later, when Peter was in his prime and his mother was no longer living, tales of his affluent life drifted back on the tongues of North Beveland sailors whose ships had docked in the distant port, and it was learned that Peter had gotten on well in the world—that he had a native valet who slept on a mat outside his room, and that he owned a villa in the country, which he had named Colijnsplaat.

But it was to their Uncle Jasper the girls turned in that fall of 1887. And when during the following winter his answer arrived inviting them to come, and offering to pay their passage, they began immediately—with the skipper's and Lavina's consent—to make preparations. Elizabeth was twenty-one now, and Leun sixteen.

On the evening before they left, the house was filled with callers—some enthusiastic and encouraging, others quiet and heavy-hearted. The heaviest heart in the house was that of Grootmoeder Betje Breas, who sat like an image of grief in her long black dress and wide white cap. She had seen both her sons sail away to spend their lives on other shores, and it cut her deeply now to relinquish these two granddaughters. But that was not all. Their going implied that the skipper and Lavina themselves hoped eventually to follow. The very thought of this, and of the emptiness she would know when the big lively family had gone, was more, almost, than she could bear. But the sorrows of Grootmoeder were lost on the two young emigrées that night. Their eyes shone with anticipation.

In the midst of the excitement and pleasant confusion a knock sounded on the door. It was a messenger who had come to say that a friend waited on the dike for Leun. The girl was surprised to be summoned so imperatively at that hour, but she made every attempt to appear casual as she left the room and stepped out into the cool March air.

In the dimness she discerned the figure of a youth on the wall directly opposite the house and knew at once it was Gilles. Did he really care so much? she asked herself as she reached the foot of the dike and began to climb.

"Leun?" came his voice, quietly.

"Yes?"

"I have come to say farewell," he explained, "and to give you—this," handing her a small package.

The occasion and the setting, and the boy who had so imaginatively chosen the hour and the place—all impressed upon the girl in her confusion the need of an equally gracious response. But she was much too excited about everything that was happening to her—including Gilles—to collect herself and take time to show more than a flicker of appreciation. She accepted the little autograph book he had brought her, thanked him, and bidding him a quick goodby turned and flew down the dike. Only Gilles himself would know how long he stood there alone in the darkness after the door closed behind her.

Next morning their Uncle Adriaan De Pree drove the girls and their father to Kortgene, where they boarded the steamer for Rotterdam.

They were off! But where was the anticipation they had felt when they planned all this? Gone, it seemed, to no one knew where. Taking leave of their mother had not been easy, and soon they would have to live through the ordeal again when they said goodby to their father.

In Rotterdam, where Elizabeth and Leun would board

a train for Amsterdam, they shopped and filled an otherwise pensive hour having photographs taken. Adriaan did his best to be matter-of-fact and cheerful, but by the time they arrived at the station his spirits had sagged, and it was fortunate for all that the train departed on schedule.

The *Zaandam* would be a trustworthy ship, he assured himself as he walked away in his solitude, and Jasper and Julia would take good care of his girls once they arrived in Grand Rapids.

The two were constantly before him as he voyaged home. Elizabeth, fair-skinned and hazel-eyed, had looked especially gentle in her olive green wool, and Leun was like a small, bright accent beside her, her piquant face and high coloring enhanced by her beige costume and the gold pin at her throat.

Through the days that followed, the skipper's heart and mind were steadfastly out on the sea. One night in a surge of feeling he sat down at the table and wrote a poem to the travelers. It was a somber poem, but filled with warmth and solicitude; and its closing lines were direct and simple:

> *One thing we, your father and mother, know—*
> *Your absence to us grief has brought;*
> *But we have learned to pray the All-protector*
> *For your safe passage on the liner to its port.*

(Translated from Dutch)

The Skipper Sails West

Spring came again to Colijnsplaat, melting the ice off the moat and ponds and bringing fresh green to the dike, the lindens, and the lilac bush on the Dorpstraat. To some the surge of light and warmth brought hope for a year of better crops and livelier trade; but for others it only increased a growing restlessness within.

With the apathy in commerce that lay like an invisible weight on the land, shipping had declined steadily, and the *Lavina,* which had sailed with such blithe regularity to Rotterdam, now spent more and more time in its berth at Colijnsplaat.

To the skipper the immediate future showed little promise of improvement. Reluctant to wait through the summer and fall to see whether the tide in his affairs would turn, he decided with Lavina to sell their house and their business as quickly as possible and follow their daughters to the United States.

Jan, nine years old, heard the news with elation; his

expectations were immediately boundless. He had been reading books about a primitive America, and he pictured a land populated mainly with cowboys and Indians. One illustration in particular had held his attention and burned itself into his memory—of a mounted Indian riding away with a white child in his arms, while pursuing him at a short distance came a cowboy, tense in his saddle and flourishing a pistol.

In one of his letters from America Jasper Breas had written his sister Lavina, "If you ever come, bring your blankets along. The winters here are cold." And Neeltje, having heard her mother read aloud this piece of advice, had visions of Siberian seasons in a land whose very name—Noord Amerika—sounded remote and glacial, like that of a place away off in the white regions of the Arctic Circle.

For their last night on the island the family of nine scattered to sleep in the homes of friends and relations. They were to leave at noon, sailing across to Zierikzee in Adriaan Karreman's ferry. From there they would take the sidewheel steamer to Rotterdam.

The great day arrived—it was late April—and long before sailing time the children gathered on the quay with a host of friends and cousins. Sailing with the Merizons would be Mr. Vander Stel, a former bakeshop owner, and his family.

It was an auspicious time to be starting out toward new beginnings. The eastern light flooded the sea and estuary with radiance, the air had lost its sharp edge, and the vivid new grass on the dike was already spangled with wild flowers. Little did Jan and his brothers know, eager as they were to be off, how their memories of this shore and this harbor would fill them with an almost unbearable nostalgia, once they had settled on strange soil far inland from the sea and the tides.

So impatient was Jan to reach the American docks and go aboard the S.S. *Rotterdam* that the ferry ride to Zierikzee

S.S. *Rotterdam*

was incidental, though at any other time it would have been a great thing. And even the prospect of traveling on the sidewheel steamer—the boat that had spouted such magnificent clouds of black smoke the first time he saw it, and whose wash had rocked the *Lavina* in the Krammer; the kind of steamer he had wanted passionately to own some day—that ride, too, was dwarfed now by the far greater events that were to follow.

All too soon for Lavina, bidding her mother a final "Dag," the call "Al an boord!" was sounded. Sails were hoisted and the anchor weighed, and the ferry amid a chorus of farewells moved away from the quay.

Once out of the harbor it headed directly for Zierikzee, three miles to the northeast across the shining strait—a course it had followed daily, year after year, and would be following for years to come. Perhaps the most wistful eyes in the party that April morning were the blue-grey eyes of Jana, looking back to the place where the fair-haired Adriaan had anchored his barge when he came to be with her those blissful holidays.

For Adriaan and Lavina, too, there was distress in relinquishing sight of that familiar shore; and to Adriaan it was like a dream to be crossing for the last time—and in another man's boat—these waters that were so much a part of him.

But in America a house was furnished and waiting. Elizabeth and Leun were already putting down roots, and old friends from Colijnsplaat awaited their coming.

Under the taut, curved sails of the ferry the travelers made good headway, and now and again they would measure with their eyes the distance to Zierikzee, where the medieval tower, dark and solitary against the luminous sky, marked their goal in the first lap of their long, hope-filled journey.

The End

Dutch Glossary

achter de kerk: Behind the church
Acterweg: street name
babelaars: sweet caramel hard candies
bellen: dial; rings
beukjes: starched white dickies for girls
bezem: a bundle of twigs tied to a stick
blauwe jannen: purple-skinned potatoes; called "blue johns"
Bomma: Grandma
Brakel: Bible
bratjes: bits of colored yarn to insert in knitting work as markers
broedertjes: the gypsies sold these little soft, flat cakes—like pancakes
buig-ijs: "bend ice"
burghers: civilians
Burgomaster: mayor
de bakker: the baker
de blijk: the bleach
de Koning's Padje: the King's Path
de Ouden Molen: the Old Mill
Dominie: pastor, preacher
gezellig: cozy, intimate
gornet: shrimp
griffel: slate pencil
Groote Kerk: the State Church; great church
grootvader: grandfather
ijs bak: "ice box," or sleigh
karrepap: oatmeal cooked in buttermilk
klapje: small blow or slap
kermis: circus

klompen: wooden shoes; clogs
kolossal: colossal; huge; prodigious
komijnekaas: spiced cheese
knicker kerk: little, small church
kralen: beads
kreukel: sea snail
krullen: spiral gold ornament for hair
lepelkost: "spoon food," one-dish meals
lezen, schrijven, rekenen, and spellen: reading, writing, arithmetic, and spelling
lijkbidder: the man who brought the message of death to village homes; in a singsong voice gave an announcement at homes of relatives and friends of the deceased.
madder: plant harvested for cloth dying
Mevrouw: Madam
middag: mid-day
Mijnheer: Mister
moe: Zeeland dialect for "aunt." Formal Dutch word is *tante*.
Moeder: mother
Mossels: mussels
pallegastepap: barley gruel
pannekoeken: pancakes
pepermunt doosje: tin/box for peppermints
pickelen: a set of small knucklebones from a pig. They were set in different positions as the game proceeded. It was played something like jacks.
Plaatjes: sole, flounder
plattekoeken: flat cakes
potlood: pencil
prikslees: little sleds that were propelled with two short poles fitted at the tips with metal points.

pruik: wig
pruime moes: prune porridge
ribbelingen: long green apples
Roompot: an area in the water just south of the Banjaard Reef periodically churned into a mass of froth.
sak: sack or bag
sardrijkskunde: earth-kingdom science; geography
shoenmakker: shoe maker
snuf doosje: pinch box; silver *snuf doosje*, its tiny enclosed sponge moist with cologne
Stadhuis: town hall
stokvis: dried fish from Scotland; very hard
stovel or stovè: a low, partially underground building where *madder* was raised for dyes
stroopvet: a butter; A mixture of pork fat and syrup
vader: father
varrekieker: hand telescope
vijver: pond
voetekot: feet warmer
Vogelgezang: birdsong
Voorstraat: main street
vroux: woman; wife
Whitsuntide: following Sunday Pentecost in the churches came two days of festival and celebration in the streets.
wijn: wine
yutten: small sugar pears
zee kraal: notched green shoots like beads connected that grew in the sea, at low tide they would be four or five inches above the sand. This vegetable could be cooked or eaten raw. A delicacy.

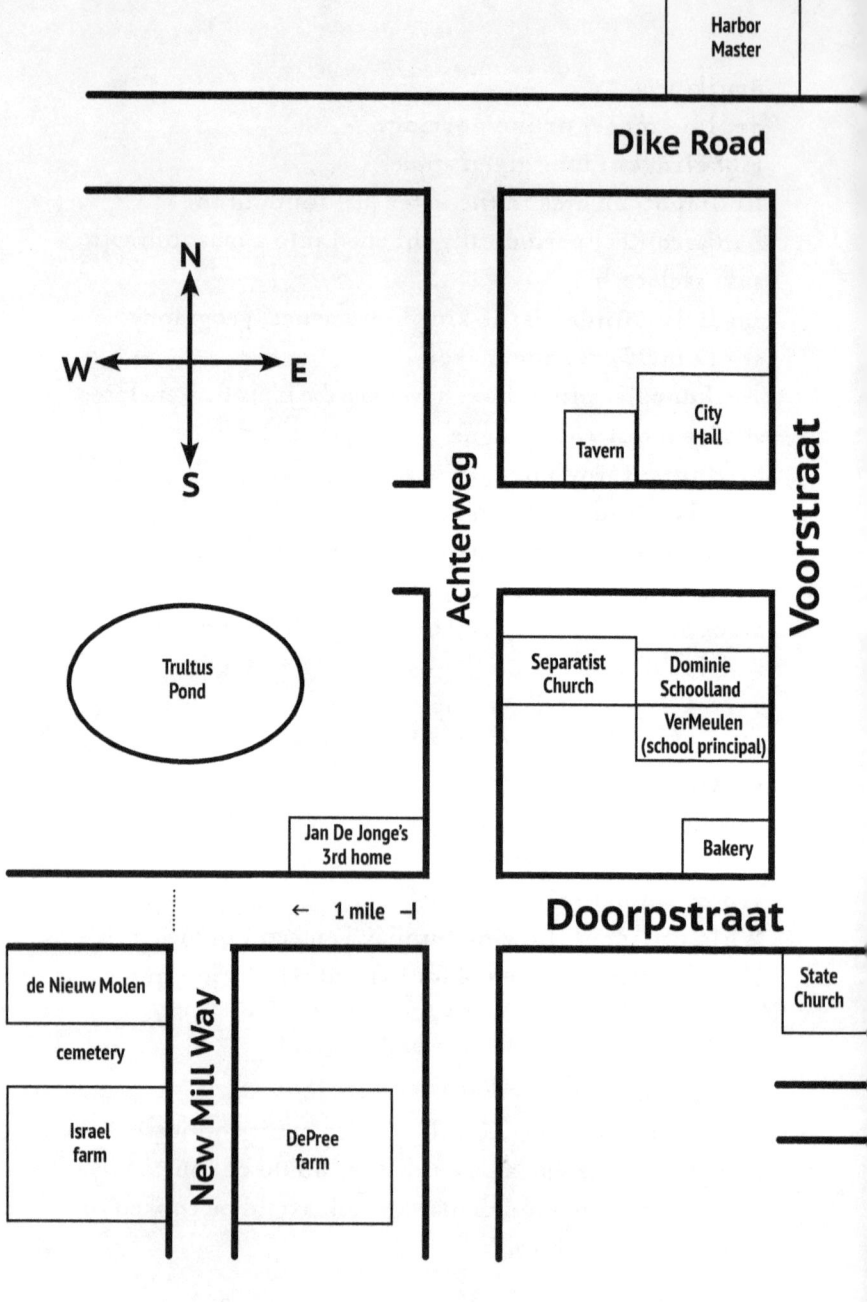

Village of Colijnsplaat

(as depicted in story and originally rendered by Sharon Merizon)

Vijver
Pond
King's Path
Hotel de Patrijs
Adriaan Merizon's 2nd home
David-Teune De Jonge
Beune (schoolmaster)
VanderStel (baker)
Dr. Berkenfeld
Achterstraat
Mill Road (Molenweg)
Adriaan Merizon's 1st home
Bieubous (burgomaster)
Vander Blouw
shop
Grastek (tax collector)
Marinus De Jonge (carriage service)
Eekman
coal shed
Koole
shop
shop
Marinus Merizon's
Jan De Jonge's 2nd home
De Oude Molen (Potappel's)
1/2 mile
Public school
Dominie van Leeuwen
moat
churchyard
Acter de Kerk
klompenmaker
Jan DeJonge's 1st home

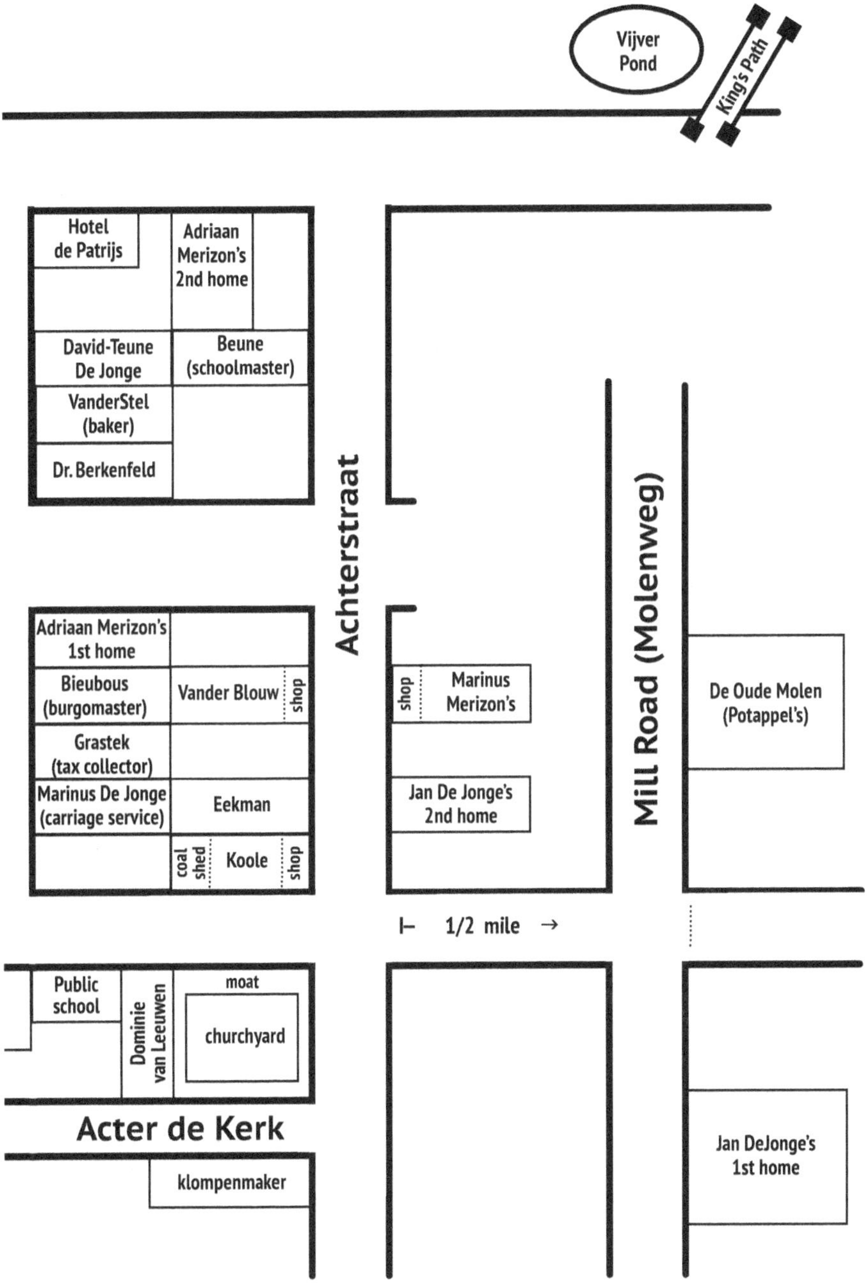

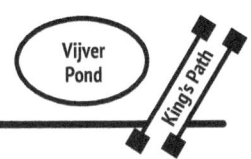

About the Author

Beth Merizon graduated from Calvin College in Grand Rapids, Michigan. She attended the University of Michigan and won the Hopwood Award for Poetry. Her first book of poems, April Trees, *was privately published in 1947. After teaching for two years, Merizon became a journalist and editor. She subsequently spent 24 years as an associate editor and senior editor at the National Union of Christian Schools. Her total involvement in the production of the magazine,* Christian Home and School, *her excellent editorial work on several major textbooks, and work on other numerous publications earned her great respect with her peers and co-workers. Merizon retired in 1973 and continued her writing and specialized editing career as a freelancer. This book is a nonfiction depiction of her parents' lives on a North Sea island village and their eventual emigration to the United States. The manuscript was a semi-finalist in the Atlantic Nonfiction Contest. She has also published numerous poems, essays and book reviews.*

Marguerite Beth Merizon
November 4, 1908—February 23, 2003

www.ingramcontent.com/pod-product-compliance
Lightning Source LLC
Chambersburg PA
CBHW022105090426
42743CB00008B/719